Quick Cooks' Kitchen

Good-Carb Recipes

Quick Cooks' Kitchen

Good-Carb Recipes

By Mary B. Johnson

BARNES
& NOBLE
BOOKS
NEW YORK

Library of Congress Cataloging-in-Publication Data Available

2 4 6 8 10 9 7 5 3

Published by Sterling Publishing Co., Inc.
387 Park Avenue South, New York, NY 10016
This book is comprised of material from the following Sterling titles:
The Ultimate Low-Carb Cookbook © 2004 by Sterling Publishing Co., Inc.
501 Recipes for a Low-Carb Life © 2003 by Sterling Publishing Co., Inc.

© 2004 by Sterling Publishing Co., Inc.
Photographs © 2004 by Theresa Raffetto

Design by Liz Trovato

Photographs by Theresa Raffetto
Food Stylist: Victoria Granof
Prop Stylist: Sharon Ryan

ISBN 0-7607-5746-1

Introduction

With so many options for a quick meal these days—quality frozen, prepped, and ready-to-heat foods; take-out and delivery; and microwavable everything—there seems to be little reason to cook! In addition, nearly all of these options are offered with a low-carb or good-carb-friendly hook. So, if you need a quick meal and are watching your carb intake you may still ask—why turn on your stove at all? Because the *Quick Cooks' Kitchen: Good-Carb Recipes* provides you with 175 recipes that are full of home-cooked goodness that satisfies the busy chef in us all.

When you think of comfort foods and home-style cooking, high carb counts are usually not far behind. The recipes in this book help you to cut carbs, but not to eliminate them. After much discussion and controversy, researchers, doctors, and nutritionists have begun to move from plans that severely restrict carb intake into a more balanced camp. "Good-carb" is now the new buzzword.

Prolonging life and preventing disease are essential factors in the consideration of a diet plan. It has been proven that excess pounds make people sluggish, lethargic, unmotivated, and generally hinder the course they need to take towards a long and healthy life. It is on this point that a plethora of current diets are providing conflicting information about what is a "healthy" way to lose and maintain weight. The Atkins, Zone, South Beach, and high-protein diets have proven that, if followed exactly, they can promote weight loss.

Still, many experts do stop short of recommending the extremely high levels of protein suggested by eating plans like the Atkins diet because these plans so drastically cut carbohydrates—the initial phase of the Atkins diet limits carbohydrates to 20 grams a day. Carbohydrates are a necessary part of a healthy diet because they provide the body with the energy it needs for physical activity and to keep organs functioning properly. Carbohydrates are the major source of fiber in the diet. Many foods rich in whole-grain carbohydrates are also good sources of essential vitamins and minerals.

Traditionally, carbohydrates that were classified as complex—such as bread, pasta, and other starches—were considered to be "good," and simple carbohydrates or sugars—such as table sugar, candy, and honey—were thought of as "bad." The "good"-"bad" distinction also applies to ingredients with naturally occurring carbs, such as fruits, vegetables, meat, and fish with varying quantities of carbs.

In this cookbook you will find recipes from a variety of cuisines—some have international origins and some are decidedly domestic. All, however, are chock full of good-carb ingredients that will satiate your hunger and not leave you feeling deprived. The portion sizes and serving suggestions try to help home cooks achieve realistic goals towards moderation in their diets. These recipes offer nutritional balance, great flavors, and will get meals on the table with speed and ease.

Quick Cooks' Tips

Throughout these pages you will come across shortcuts, hints, and tips that are designed to help you. Here is some general advice to always consider when you are in the kitchen:

• Always read the recipe from start to finish before beginning your preparation. Make sure you understand the directions and reread anything that seems unclear to you.

• Start by getting all of your ingredients within reach and do all of your prep work before beginning to cook.

Basic Tools

You can create any of the recipes in this book with just a few basic kitchen tools.

Cutting board: At least one board in either wood or plastic is a must-have. Whichever you choose, be sure to get one large enough for unhindered chopping, yet small enough for easy washing. For food safety, remember to use separate boards (or separate sides of one board) for cutting produce and raw meats and to wash the boards thoroughly between uses.

Chef's knife: Select a top-quality knife and keep it sharp for optimum performance. This knife comes in 6-, 8-, 10-, and 12-inch lengths. The 8-inch one gets our vote for versatility. It lets you cut meats, chop vegetables, and mince garlic and herbs in no time flat.

Paring knife: A paring knife usually comes with a 3- or 4-inch blade and makes short work of trimming mushrooms, peeling fruits, and other similar tasks.

Vegetable peeler: This tool is ideal for peeling thin-skinned root vegetables such as carrots, potatoes, parsnips, and even young butternut squash. Find a peeler with a swivel blade and a comfortable handle.

Measuring cups and spoons: Get a nested set of dry measuring cups for measuring rice, pasta, beans, and frozen peas and corn. Use a liquid measure for broth, tomatoes, and other liquid ingredients. The same set of nested spoons can be used for dry and wet items.

Wooden spoons: Wooden spoons are good for most mixing and stirring tasks. They don't scratch pots, pans, or dishes, and their shallow bowls are perfectly suited for stirring. Their handles stay cool, and don't melt if you accidentally leave them touching a hot pot.

Saucepans and pots: The saucepan is the smaller of the two and has one handle; the pot is larger and has two handles. The pot, however, will give you more room for stirring and gentle simmering. Make sure you get a snug-fitting lid for whatever you have.

Immersion blender: This handy gadget allows you to purée ingredients directly in the pot. If you don't have one, a blender, food processor, food mill, or potato masher will work.

And, last but not least, make sure you have a trusty can opener!

Appetizers & Snacks

Avocado Cocktail

MAKES 4 SERVINGS

Who needs shrimp when you can concentrate on a perfectly ripe avocado? The sauce is versatile and easy to prepare.

SAUCE:

4 ounces whipped cream cheese, softened
2 pickled jalapeños, chopped, and a little juice
1/4 cup spicy tomato juice

1 avocado
1 tablespoon fresh lemon juice
salt to taste
freshly ground pepper to taste
1 cup shredded iceberg lettuce
paprika for dusting
1 green onion, trimmed, finely chopped or shredded

● Make sauce: Whisk together cheese, peppers, and 1 teaspoon pickle juice in bowl until loosened. Whisk in tomato juice. Taste; add more pickle juice if desired. Cover; set aside until serving.

● To serve: Cut avocado in half, remove pit, and scoop out flesh onto a cutting board. Cut into bite-size chunks. Place in bowl; toss with lemon juice, salt, and pepper. Drop lettuce into 4 martini glasses or goblets; top with avocado mixture. Spoon sauce over avocado; dust with paprika. Sprinkle with onions.

Per Serving: 139 calories, 5g carbohydrates, 4g protein, 13g fat

PREP TIME: 15 MINUTES   COOKING TIME: NONE

Prosciutto di Parma Rolls

MAKES 24 ROLLS (6 SERVINGS)

*6 thin (but thicker than paper-thin) slices prosciutto
 di Parma*
*1 (5-ounce) package pepper-flavored imported soft
 cheese, at room temperature*
24 (2-inch) lengths fresh asparagus tips

● Spread out prosciutto slices onto cutting board. Using pizza cutter, cut prosciutto crosswise and then lengthwise in half.

● Place cheese on sheet of parchment. Top with another sheet of parchment. With rolling pin, flatten to a 6 x 4-inch rectangle. Remove top sheet; press through cheese with a long thin skewer to cut into 24 pieces (4 times crosswise, 6 times lengthwise.)

● Spoon cheese portion onto one end of each prosciutto strip. Top with an asparagus spear. Roll up from cheese end.

Per serving: 131 calories, 7g carbohydrates,
10g protein, 8g fat

Beef Carpaccio with Grilled Asparagus & Parmesan Crisps

MAKES 6 SERVINGS

This is an involved creation—but great for entertaining because each part can be done ahead and then assembled for serving. The raw beef is a flavorful and textural contrast to the juicy asparagus, crisp cheese wafers, and rich egg sauce. And the fresh lemon juice and shredded basil shine through as aromatic and palate-pleasing accents.

12 ounces beef tenderloin or boneless sirloin steak
1 pound medium-thick asparagus spears
olive oil for brushing
salt and pepper

SAUCE
1 tablespoon red wine vinegar
3 eggs
4 scallions, trimmed and finely chopped
1 garlic clove, very finely chopped (optional)
2 tablespoons extra-virgin olive oil
salt and freshly ground pepper to taste

FOR SERVING
olive oil
juice of 1/2 lemon
sea salt and pepper
Parmesan Crisps (recipe follows)
6 fresh basil leaves, shredded

• Cut the beef into paper-thin slices. Line 6 flat plates with plastic wrap and divide the beef among the plates, arranging the slices in one layer to more or less cover the centers of the plates. Cover with plastic wrap. Invert each plastic-wrap-encased beef packet onto the work surface and pound gently with a flat meat mallet or rolling pin until the beef is very thin. Remove the top layers of plastic wrap and cover each with one of the plates. Using the plastic wrap, lift up the beef onto the plate and quickly flip over the plate to invert the beef onto it. Set aside or refrigerate until ready to serve.

• Snap off the tough ends from the asparagus spears and discard. Peel spears if desired. Cook in boiling salted water for 3 minutes or until just tender but still quite firm. Drain and place in a bowl of ice water until completely cold. Drain the asparagus again and pat dry on a paper-towel-lined baking sheet. Brush with oil and sprinkle with salt and pepper. Heat a grill pan until very hot; cook asparagus to mark with grill lines, about 3 minutes.

• For the sauce: Place the vinegar in a small pan of simmering salted water, then poach the eggs until the whites are firm and the yolks are just cooked through. Drain and place in a bowl of ice cold water to stop the

cooking. Drain on paper towels. Place the poached eggs in a medium bowl and crush to a fine consistency with a fork. Add the scallions, garlic, oil, salt, and pepper, and mix well. Set aside.

• To serve: Remove the plastic wrap from the plates and brush the beef with olive oil. Sprinkle with the lemon juice and season with sea salt and pepper. Place a Parmesan Crisp on top of each carpaccio, then add the grilled asparagus and sprinkle with basil. Spoon the egg sauce around and serve.

Per serving (without the Parmesan Crisps): 301 calories, 5g carbohydrates, 18g protein, 23g fat.

PREP TIME: 5 MINUTES   COOKING TIME: 6 MINUTES

Parmesan Crisps

Makes 16 servings

olive oil for brushing
3/4 cup freshly grated Parmesan cheese
salt and freshly ground black pepper to taste

• Place an 8-inch nonstick skillet over low heat, brush with a film of olive oil and then sprinkle with a thin, even layer of Parmesan. Sprinkle with salt and pepper. Cook for about 2 minutes or until the cheese melts and turns golden. Use a metal spatula to transfer the Crisps to paper towels. Repeat to make 6 Crisps in all.

Per serving: 77 calories, trace carbohydrates, 5g protein, 6g fat

PREP TIME: 5 MINUTES   COOKING TIME: NONE

Sliced Mushrooms with Lemon Vinaigrette

MAKES 4 SERVINGS

finely shredded zest and juice of 1 lemon
3 tablespoons extra-virgin olive oil for drizzling
kosher salt and freshly ground black pepper
8 ounces sliced small white mushrooms (buy them
  already sliced)
wedge of Parmiagiano-Reggiano cheese

● Mix lemon zest and juice, oil, and salt and pepper in medium bowl until blended. Add mushrooms; toss to coat. Place on flat serving plate. Shred curls of Parmiagiano-Reggiano on top.

Per serving: 132 calories, 4g carbohydrates, 4g protein, 12g fat

PREP TIME: 5 MINUTES   COOKING TIME: 5 MINUTES

Mushrooms on Toast

MAKES 4 SERVINGS

This is a tasty, quick appetizer or first course that is basically foolproof. The sauce is simply wine and cream mixed with the juices of the mushrooms.

1 teaspoon butter
3 ounces sliced mushrooms
1 tablespoon dry white wine
1/4 cup half-and-half
2 scallions, trimmed and finely chopped
1 tablespoon chopped fresh dill
1 thin slice white bread, toasted, cut diagonally
  into quarters

● Melt the butter in a medium nonstick skillet over medium-high heat. Add the mushrooms and cook for 2 to 3 minutes.

● Add the white wine and reduce the liquid slightly. Add the half-and-half, scallions, and dill. Serve on hot toast points.

Per serving: 48 calories, 4g carbohydrates, 1g protein, 3g fat

QUICK COOKS' TIP:

Only cook with wine good enough for you to drink. If you use anything sub-par, the taste will be evident in your dish.

PREP TIME: 10 MINUTES   COOKING TIME: 10 MINUTES

Toasted Shrimp Appetizers

MAKES 2 DOZEN APPETIZERS

These are a baked version of the classic Chinese deep-fried appetizer: shrimp toasts.

8 ounces medium unpeeled shrimp
1 garlic clove, peeled
2 scallions, cut into 1-inch pieces
1 1/2 teaspoons cornstarch
1 1/2 teaspoons dry sherry
1 egg white
1/2 cup sliced, peeled fresh or canned water chestnuts
24 slices party-style rye bread
1/4 cup bottled sweet and sour sauce

• Preheat the oven to 375 degrees. Peel and devein the shrimp and set aside.

• Position the knife blade in the food processor bowl. With the processor running, drop the garlic through the food chute and process until minced. Add the scallions and process until chopped. Add the cornstarch, sherry, and egg white and process until well blended. Add the shrimp and water chestnuts and pulse until finely chopped.

• Spread about 1 tablespoon of the shrimp mixture over each bread slice and place spread side up on a baking sheet. Bake until shrimp mixture is cooked through, about 10 minutes.

Per serving (serving size: 1 appetizer & 1/2 teaspoon sauce): 33 calories, 5g carbohydrates, 3g protein, trace fat

Herb Pancakes

MAKES 12 SERVINGS

These thin Italian pancakes are traditionally served the way the French often eat their crêpes—layered with a filling in between them or rolled around a filling.

1 cup unsifted all-purpose flour

4 eggs

3 tablespoons butter, melted

sea salt to taste

1³/4 cups water

1 cup coarsely chopped mixed fresh herbs, ideally
    fennel feather, basil, and parsley

sunflower oil for deep frying

freshly grated Parmesan cheese for serving

• Combine the flour, eggs, 1³/4 cups water, and half the melted butter and a dash of salt in a blender and blend until smooth. Pour into a bowl and stir in the herbs. After adding the remaining butter, make large pancakes with the batter in a large nonstick skillet. When the pancakes are cool, cut them into tagliatelle-size (about ³/4-inch-wide) strips.

• Deep-fry the pancake strips, in batches, in sunflower oil for a couple of minutes, until crisp. Serve hot with grated Parmesan and sea salt.

Per serving: 110 calories, 9g carbohydrates, 4g protein, 6g fat

QUICK COOKS' TIP:

Now that you have cut the pancakes like pasta—use them like pasta. Top the herb "noodles" with your favorite store-bought pasta sauce. Serve with a side salad and you will have a delicious, satisfying good-carb dinner.

PREP TIME: 15 MINUTES   COOKING TIME: 3 MINUTES

Baba Ganoush

MAKES 8 SERVINGS

This roasted eggplant dip is a Middle Eastern specialty.

4 tablespoons olive oil

2 medium eggplants

salt and pepper

1 large tomato, finely diced

1 handful fresh mint leaves, chopped

1 garlic clove, crushed

1 1/2 tablespoons fresh lemon juice

• Preheat the broiler. Line a baking sheet with aluminum foil and grease with half the olive oil. Slice the eggplant crosswise into 1/4-inch slices and place on the prepared baking sheet. Turn them over so the oiled side is up. Sprinkle with salt and pepper and broil until charred, 2 to 3 minutes. Repeat on the other side with the remaining oil and eggplant.

• Using a blender, purée the eggplant with the tomato, mint, lemon juice, and garlic.

Per serving: 48 calories, 4g carbohydrates, 1g protein, 4g fat

QUICK COOKS' TIP:

Although this is traditionally served as an appetizer, Baba Ganoush goes great as a side dish with grilled lamb and is hearty enough to serve as a sandwich filling in pita bread.

PREP TIME: 12 MINUTES   COOKING TIME: 8 MINUTES

Crispy Tofu Cubes with Asian Lime Dipping Sauce

MAKES 4 SERVINGS

12 ounces firm tofu

SAUCE

2 green onions, trimmed, thinly sliced

1/4 cup fresh lime juice

1 tablespoon honey

1/4 cup Vietnamese or Thai fish sauce (nuoc mam or nam pla) or light soy sauce

1/4 cup water

1 teaspoon Chinese garlic-chili sauce or sambal oelek, or to taste

1 1/4 cups peanut oil or vegetable oil for frying

• Drain tofu; wrap in triple-thickness paper towels and place in shallow bowl. Weight down with a heavy can or skillet. Let stand 10 minutes, changing paper towels after 5 minutes if they are soaked.

• While tofu drains, mix sauce ingredients in a bowl.

• Heat oil in deep saucepan or wok until shimmering. Cut tofu into 1-inch cubes; fry, in batches, until golden, about 4 minutes per batch. Drain on paper towels; serve with sauce for dipping.

Per serving: 158 calories, 10g carbohydrates, 8g protein, 11g fat

**PREP TIME: 10 MINUTES   MARINATING TIME: 2 HOURS
COOKING TIME: 8 MINUTES**

Shrimp Steamed in Ginger-Sake Broth

MAKES 6 SERVINGS

1/2 cup sake

4 tablespoons chopped peeled fresh gingerroot

1 1/2 pounds medium shrimp, shelled and deveined

1/4 cup soy sauce

1/4 cup rice vinegar

1/4 cup mirin (sweet rice wine) or dry sherry

1/2 teaspoon salt to taste

3 tablespoons snipped fresh chives

● Heat 1/4 cup sake and 2 tablespoons ginger to boiling in skillet over medium-high heat. Add shrimp; spread out. Cover; reduce heat to medium. Steam until shrimp are pink and barely cooked through (do not overcook). Drain; cool.

● While shrimp cool, mix soy sauce and remaining ginger in small skillet. Simmer until soy sauce is reduced to 1 tablespoon. Add remaining 1/4 cup sake and 2 tablespoons ginger, the vinegar, mirin, and salt. Mix well.

● Place shrimp in bowl; pour soy sauce mixture over shrimp. Toss to coat. Cover and refrigerate at least 2 hours, stirring every 30 minutes.

● To serve: Remove shrimp from marinade with slotted spoon; arrange on serving plate. Sprinkle with chives.

Per serving: 213 calories, 8g carbohydrates, 24g protein, 5g fat

PREP TIME: 10 MINUTES   COOKING TIME: 4 MINUTES

Guacamole Japonaise with Pot-Sticker Chips

MAKES 6 SERVINGS

The rich avocado mixture we flavor with a Mexican accent is just as delicious seasoned with the elements that go into sushi. Hot gingerroot, spicy seasoned rice vinegar, and fiery wasabi pack just as powerful a punch as a mix of chilies.

1 tablespoon black or white sesame seeds
1 large firm, ripe avocado
1 tablespoon shredded pickled ginger
3 tablespoons seasoned rice vinegar or 3 tablespoons
  cider vinegar, mixed with 1 teaspoon sugar
1/2 teaspoon wasabi powder or prepared horseradish
Pot-Sticker Chips for dipping (recipe follows)

• Place the sesame seeds in a small skillet over medium-high heat. Shake pan often until seeds begin to pop, 3 to 4 minutes. Pour the seeds into a bowl and set aside to cool.

• Cut the avocado in half and remove the pit. Scoop out the flesh from the peel and dice into small pieces. Place the avocado in a bowl and add 1/2 teaspoon sesame seeds, the ginger, vinegar, and wasabi. Stir gently to mix. Transfer to a serving bowl and sprinkle with the remaining sesame seeds. Serve as a dip, with the Pot-Sticker Chips.

Per serving (without the Pot-Sticker Chips): 49 calories, 2g carbohydrates, 1g protein, 5g fat

PREP TIME: 5 MINUTES   COOKING TIME: 8 MINUTES

Pot-Sticker Chips

MAKES 4 SERVINGS

You can make the chips ahead and store them at room temperature in an airtight container up to 2 days before serving.

nonstick cooking spray
12 round pot-sticker skins

• Preheat the oven to 450 degrees. Grease a large baking sheet with nonstick cooking spray. Dip the pot-sticker skins one at a time in a bowl of water, shake off the excess, and place in a single layer on the prepared baking sheet. Bake until browned and crisp, 4 to 8 minutes, depending on the thickness of the skins. Cool on wire racks.

Per chip: 23 calories, 5g carbohydrates, 1g protein, trace fat

QUICK COOKS' TIP:

Wasabi powder and paste can be found at Asian groceries, specialty food stores, and now at most major supermarkets.

PREP TIME: 10 MINUTES   COOKING TIME: 7 TO 9 MINUTES

Crunchy Pecan Chicken Fingers

MAKES 5 SERVINGS

Dip these babies into a sweet-and-sour sauce or drizzle with honey mustard. They are even great just wrapped in a hot soft dinner roll for a soup-and-sandwich supper.

1/2 cup finely chopped pecans
1/3 cup cornflake crumbs
1 tablespoon chopped fresh parsley
1 tablespoon grated lemon rind
1/8 teaspoon salt
1/8 teaspoon garlic powder
1/4 cup skim milk
12 ounces skinless, boneless chicken-breast halves

• Preheat the oven to 400 degrees. Line a baking sheet with aluminum foil.

• Combine the pecans, cornflake crumbs, parsley, lemon rind, salt, and garlic powder in a shallow bowl. Place the milk on a plate. Cut the chicken breasts into 3-inch by 1-inch strips. Dip the chicken pieces into the milk, drain off the excess, and then roll in the crumb mixture. Place the chicken on the prepared baking pan and bake until tender and no longer pink, 7 to 9 minutes.

Per serving: 172 calories, 5g carbohydrates, 18g protein, 9g fat

PREP TIME: 10 MINUTES   COOKING TIME: NONE

Ham-Wrapped Mango

MAKES 4 SERVINGS

The sweet and juicy tropical fruit is the perfect mate for the salty ham.

1 firm ripe mango
2 ounces thinly sliced prosciutto
lime wedges for garnish

• Cut the mango in half lengthwise around the pit on one side; slice out pit. Score flesh into 1-inch gridlike pattern without tearing skin. Push on skin so mango cubes pop out; cut off into a bowl.

• Stack prosciutto slices; cut lengthwise with pizza cutter into long 2-inch strips. Wrap each slice around a piece of mango and secure with wooden picks. Place on a serving dish with lime wedges for squeezing.

Per serving: 62 calories, 10g carbohydrates, 3g protein, 2g fat

Zucchini-Stuffed Mushrooms

MAKES 18 STUFFED MUSHROOMS

Stuffed mushrooms are a classic cocktail party hors d'oeuvre—but these are served up with a taste twist—and are low in carbs!

18 large mushrooms, cleaned and trimmed
1¹/2 tablespoon extra-virgin olive oil, divided,
    plus more for greasing dish
1 tablespoon dry white wine
1 large garlic clove, crushed through a press
1 medium zucchini (8 ounces), finely chopped
1/4 cup grated Asiago or provolone cheese
salt, freshly ground pepper, and dried oregano
    leaves to taste

- Preheat broiler. Grease a shallow 2-quart baking dish with oil.

- Remove mushroom stems; finely chop. Heat 1 tablespoon oil in large skillet over medium heat; add mushroom caps; sauté 3 minutes. Add wine and sauté 3 minutes, until caps start to soften but are still firm in center. Place caps stem side up in baking dish.

- Heat remaining oil in skillet, add garlic, and sauté 30 seconds. Add mushroom stems and zucchini and sauté 3 minutes, until crisp and tender. Remove from heat; stir in cheese and seasonings to taste. Spoon mixture into caps, dividing evenly. Broil 8 inches from heat source until cheese melts, about 3 minutes.

Per serving: 24 calories, 1g carbohydrates, 1g protein, 2g fat

QUICK COOKS' TIP:

You can vary the cheese and herb mix as you wish. Gruyère is nice with thyme; Gorgonzola, with chopped fennel seeds.

PREP TIME: 12 MINUTES   COOKING TIME: 7 MINUTES

Olive & Tomato Crostini

MAKES 8 SERVINGS

olive oil nonstick cooking spray

8 (1/4-inch-thick) baguette slices

1/4 cup sun-dried tomatoes (not oil-packed)

1/2 cup pitted Calamata olives

6 leaves fresh basil, torn into small pieces

1 teaspoon extra-virgin olive oil

1/2 teaspoon finely chopped garlic

salt to taste

freshly ground pepper to taste

- Preheat the oven to 400 degrees. Lightly coat a baking sheet with cooking spray. Arrange the baguette slices on the baking sheet, lightly coat with olive oil spray, and bake for about 7 minutes, or until the toasts are golden and crisp. Let cool completely on the baking sheet.

- In a small bowl, soak the sun-dried tomatoes in the boiling water until plump, about 10 minutes. Drain well.

- In a mini-processor, combine the sun-dried tomatoes, olives, basil, olive oil, and garlic and pulse until finely chopped but not puréed. Transfer to a small bowl and season with salt and pepper. Spread each bread slice with 1 tablespoon of the olive mixture and serve.

Per serving: 53 calories, 8g carbohydrates, 1g protein, 2g fat

PREP TIME: 10 MINUTES   MARINATING TIME: 30 MINUTES   COOKING TIME: 15 MINUTES

Chinese Pork Dumplings

MAKES 20 DUMPLINGS

8 ounces lean ground pork

1 cup shredded Napa cabbage

1 scallion, trimmed and chopped

1 tablespoon soy sauce

salt and pepper to taste

20 wonton wrappers

1 egg, beaten

lettuce leaves for lining steamers

1 teaspoon dark sesame oil

bottled or homemade dipping sauce

• Combine the pork, cabbage, scallion, and soy sauce in a small bowl. Season with salt and pepper and marinate 30 minutes.

• Brush the edges of each wrapper with a little beaten egg. Place a little of the pork mixture in the center of each and fold over the wrappers, pushing the filling into the center and pushing out any trapped air. Seal the edges well.

• Place the lettuce leaves in the bottom of a steamer and place the wontons on top. Steam for 10 to 15 minutes, turning halfway through cooking and brushing with sesame oil. Serve with your choice of dipping sauce.

Per serving: 46 calories, 5g carbohydrates, 4g protein, 1g fat

QUICK COOKS' TIP:

There are many bottled dipping sauces that complement these tasty appetizers, but equal portions of soy sauce, water, and rice vinegar work fine. Add some chopped scallion and minced, peeled fresh gingerroot and you have all you need to accent the sweet filling of pork and cabbage.

Cajun Spice Rub

MAKES ABOUT 1/4 CUP

You can prepare a spice jar full of this mixture to have on hand for big jobs like a pork loin or brisket. This recipe is enough for about 6 small fish fillets or boneless pork chops.

1 tablespoons sweet Hungarian paprika

2 teaspoons salt

1 teaspoon onion powder

1 teaspoon garlic powder

1 teaspoon cayenne pepper

3/4 teaspoon freshly ground white pepper

3/4 teaspoon freshly ground black pepper

1/2 teaspoon dried thyme leaves

1/2 teaspoon dried oregano leaves

1/2 teaspoon crushed fennel seeds

1/2 teaspoon celery salt

● Mix ingredients in small bowl, using back of a spoon to break up any little lumps. Store, tightly covered, in a jar.

Each teaspoon: 5 calories, 1g carbohydrates, trace protein, trace fat

Goat Cheese Quesadilla

MAKES 24 SERVINGS

8 (6-inch) flour tortillas

4 ounces goat cheese, softened

4 small scallions, thinly sliced

freshly ground pepper to taste

2 tablespoons vegetable oil

kosher salt

Tomato-Olive Salsa for serving (recipe follows)

• Cut the tortillas into 4-inch rounds, using a small saucer as a template. Spread the tortillas with the goat cheese and sprinkle with the scallions and pepper; sandwich to make 4 quesadillas.

• In a large skillet, heat the vegetable oil. Add the quesadillas and cook over medium-high heat until golden and crisp, about 1 minute per side. Transfer the quesadillas to a cutting board and cut each one into 6 wedges. Sprinkle with salt and top each wedge with 1 teaspoon of the salsa. Serve immediately, passing the remaining salsa separately.

Per serving: 62 calories, 6g carbohydrates, 2g protein, 3g fat

Tomato-Olive Salsa

MAKES 8 SERVINGS

3 large plum tomatoes, seeded and finely chopped

1/8 teaspoon kosher salt

1/3 cup Calamata olives, pitted and finely chopped

1 tablespoon finely chopped fresh flat-leaf parsley

1 tablespoon finely chopped red onion

1 tablespoon balsamic vinegar

2 teaspoons fresh lime juice

1 teaspoon hot sauce

1/2 teaspoon minced garlic

1/4 teaspoon dried oregano leaves (preferably Mediterranean)

• In a strainer set in the sink, toss the tomatoes with the salt and let drain for 10 minutes. Transfer the tomatoes to a bowl and add the olives, parsley, onion, vinegar, lime juice, hot sauce, garlic, and oregano. Mix well.

Per serving: 144 calories, 12g carbohydrates, 2g protein, 11g fat

Grilled Smoked-Mozzarella with Zucchini

MAKES 6 SERVINGS

The smoked flavors of the cheese, zucchini, and sauce make this first course one to have all summer. You can roast and skin a batch of peppers at a time and have them individually packed in the freezer, waiting for use.

1 (7-ounce) jar roasted red peppers, drained, roughly
  chopped

1/2 cup canned diced tomatoes

1/4 cup extra-virgin olive oil

1 small garlic clove, chopped

salt and pepper to taste

1 pound smoked mozzarella

1 large zucchini, sliced lengthwise into 8 pieces

4 tablespoons aged balsamic vinegar

18 large basil leaves, deep-fried until crisp

• Prepare a charcoal grill for barbecuing. Oil the grill rack.

• Combine the pepper, tomato, oil, and garlic in a blender and pulse until smooth. Transfer to a bowl and season with salt and pepper. Set aside.

• Cut the mozzarella into 8 wedges and wrap each with a slice of zucchini. Cook the wrapped cheese on the grill over hot coals for 2 minutes on each side.

• Spoon the pepper sauce onto 8 plates and drizzle each portion with 1/2 tablespoon balsamic vinegar. Place 2 fried basil leaves and 1 grilled wrapped cheese on each plate and serve.

Per serving: 234 calories, 3g carbohydrates, 12g protein, 19g fat

Buffalo Chicken Wings
MAKES 6 SERVINGS

There doesn't seem to be a bad version of these in existence. These are nice and spicy and beautifully glazed. The dipping sauce is the best!

12 chicken wings (about 2 pounds)
3 tablespoons Louisiana hot sauce
2 tablespoons olive oil
1/4 cup Cajun Spice Rub (recipe on page 29)
1 cup Blue Cheese Dressing (recipe follows)
4 large celery stalks, trimmed, cut into 3-inch lengths

• Preheat oven to 400 degrees. Line large roasting pan with heavy-duty aluminum foil. Cut through wings at joints; discard wing tips. Place wings in prepared pan. Add 2 tablespoons hot sauce and the oil; toss to coat. Sprinkle with spice rub; toss to mix well.

• Spread wings in single layer. Roast 30 minutes; turn wings. Roast 15 to 20 minutes, until cooked through.

• Preheat broiler. Line baking sheet with heavy-duty foil. Using tongs, lift flat portion of wings from roasting pan and arrange on prepared baking sheet. Drizzle with half the remaining hot sauce; toss to coat. Broil until browned and crisp, turning once. Remove to serving dish. Repeat with drumstick portions. Serve with dressing and celery.

Note: Wings can marinate in sauce and spice rub in a zip-top plastic food storage bag in refrigerator up to 1 day in advance of cooking.

Per serving: 382 calories, 7g carbohydrates, 21g protein, 30g fat

Blue Cheese Dressing

MAKES 1 QUART

You can now call this classic and delicious blue cheese dressing recipe your very own.

2 cups mayonnaise

8 ounces Roquefort cheese, crumbled

6 ounces evaporated milk

1/4 cup fresh lemon juice

1 tablespoon chopped fresh parsley

2 tablespoons distilled white vinegar

1 teaspoon garlic salt

dash celery seed

● Mix ingredients together in a bowl until blended.

Per ounce: 90 calories, 4g carbohydrates, 2g protein, 7g fat

Spicy Cheese Puffs

MAKES 4 SERVINGS

Vegetable oil for frying

2 egg whites

2/3 cup grated Asiago or dry (aged) Monterey Jack cheese

1/2 teaspoon freshly ground pepper

pinch of cayenne pepper

● Heat 2 inches of oil in wide sauté pan or saucepan to 375 degrees. Meanwhile, whisk egg whites until foamy and evenly broken up. Whisk in cheese and pepper. When oil is hot, fry teaspoonfuls of egg-white mixture until puffed and brown, about 2 minutes. Drain on paper towels and serve immediately.

Per serving: 100 calories, 1g carbohydrates, 7g protein, 7.5g fat

PREP TIME: 5 MINUTES COOKING TIME: 8 MINUTES

Chicken Spedini (Kebabs)

MAKES 4 SERVINGS

16 (1-inch chunks) skinless, boneless chicken breasts
   (from 2 large breast halves)
1/4 cup balsamic vinaigrette
16 small sage leaves
4 thin slices pancetta, quartered

• Prepare outdoor grill for barbecue or preheat broiler. Place chicken cubes and vinaigrette in bowl; toss to coat. Thread chicken, sage, and pancetta onto thin metal skewers.

• Place skewers on grill rack over medium-hot coals or on rack in broiler pan 6 inches from heat source. Grill, covered if possible, or broil until cooked through, turning every 2 minutes, about 8 minutes in all.

Per serving: 346 calories, trace carbohydrates, 17g protein, 30g fat

PREP TIME: 5 MINUTES COOKING TIME: 5 MINUTES

Lemon Quail

MAKES 4 SERVINGS

4 whole quail, backbone and 2 outer wing joints
   removed
1/2 cup citrus vinaigrette
1 teaspoon dried oregano
lemon wedges for serving

• Prepare outdoor grill for barbecue or preheat broiler. Place quail breast side down on cutting board; open out and press with palm of hand to flatten. Mix vinaigrette and oregano; brush some over skin.

• Place quail skin side down on grill rack or skin side up on broiler rack in broiler pan. Grill or broil over hot coals or 4 inches from heat source until skin is browned, about 2 minutes. Cover grill if possible; grill or broil until cooked through, about 3 minutes longer. Turn quail and cook until brown inside, about 2 minutes. Serve with lemon wedges.

Per serving: 353 calories, 2g carbohydrates, 21g protein, 29g fat

Grilled Shrimp with Mint Dipping Sauce

MAKES 4 SERVINGS

8 *strips applewood-smoked bacon*

16 *jumbo shrimp, shelled, deveined, tails intact*

2 *tablespoons torn fresh mint leaves*

2 *tablespoons extra-virgin olive oil (Spanish, if available)*

2 *tablespoons sherry vinegar*

2 *tablespoons orange juice*

● Prepare outdoor grill for barbecue or preheat broiler. Cut bacon strips in half crosswise; wrap one half around each shrimp. Secure with short thin metal skewers or the pins used in roasting a turkey. Place on grill rack or rack in broiler pan; grill, covered, until bacon is crisp and shrimp is barely cooked through, about 8 minutes, turning every 2 to 3 minutes.

● While shrimp cooks, whisk mint with oil, vinegar, and orange juice in small bowl. Use as a dipping sauce for shrimp.

Per serving: 389 calories, 2g carbohydrates, 12g protein, 37g fat

Soups

Hearty Vegetable Soup with Pesto

MAKES 4 SERVINGS

1 tablespoon olive oil

1/2 cup chopped celery

2 garlic cloves, crushed through a press

6 cups chicken broth

1 (10-ounce) package frozen mixed vegetables

1 small zucchini, trimmed, diced

1/4 cup prepared or homemade pesto

• Heat oil in 3-quart saucepan over medium-high heat. Add celery and garlic; cover and steam 3 minutes. Add broth; heat to boiling. Add mixed vegetables; heat to boiling. Add zucchini; cook until vegetables are tender, about 4 minutes. Stir in pesto.

Per serving 196 calories, 13 g carbohydrate, 2g protein, 11g fat

---

QUICK COOKS' TIP:

Bouillon cubes are a fine alternative to canned broth.

Baby Carrot and Ginger Soup

MAKES 4 SERVINGS

12 ounces peeled baby carrots

3 cups chicken broth

1 tablespoon grated fresh peeled gingerroot

salt and ground white pepper to taste

1/4 cup sour cream

snipped fresh chervil, dill, or chives or a mixture of all

• Combine carrots, 1/2 cup broth, and ginger in microwave-safe bowl or saucepan. Cover; cook on high power or boil over medium-high heat until tender, 10 to 12 minutes. Place carrots and liquid in food processor or blender; purée. Place in saucepan with remaining broth. Heat to boiling. Season with salt and pepper. Serve in bowls, with dollops of sour cream and sprinkled with herbs.

Per serving: 92 calories, 10g carbohydrates, 5g protein, 4g fat

PREP TIME: 5 MINUTES   COOKING TIME: 15 MINUTES

Creamy Broccoli and Cheddar Soup

MAKES 4 SERVINGS

1 tablespoon olive oil

1 small onion, chopped

1 large garlic clove, crushed through a press

5 cups water

2 tablespoons soy sauce

1 1/4 pounds broccoli florets

freshly ground pepper to taste

2 cups shredded cheddar cheese

• Heat oil in 3-quart saucepan over medium-high heat. Add onion; sauté 3 minutes. Add garlic; sauté 1 minute. Add water and soy sauce; heat to boiling. Add broccoli; cook until tender, about 8 minutes. Remove 4 florets; rinse in strainer with cold water and set aside for garnish.

• Drain soup through colander, reserving broth. Purée solids in food processor or blender, adding enough reserved broth to assist puréeing. Add cheese; purée until melted. Return broth to pan; stir in purée; heat to boiling. Season with pepper. Ladle into bowls. Add one reserved floret to each for garnish.

Per serving: 306 calories, 10g carbohydrates, 19g protein, 23g fat

PREP TIME: 5 MINUTES   COOKING TIME: 10 MINUTES

Quick Beet & Sour Cream Soup

6 SERVINGS

This is the easiest beet soup you may ever make. It relies on the sweetness of the earthy vegetable balancing the acidity of the rich sour cream.

6 peeled beets

1 tablespoon sugar

1 1/4 cups sour cream

1 tablespoon all-purpose flour

1 egg yolk

1 cup croutons

• Place 3 of the beets in a food processor and purée. Transfer to a 2-quart saucepan. Chop the remaining beets and add to the puréed beets. Add 5 cups water and the sugar. Heat to boiling and simmer until the beets are tender, about 10 minutes.

• Meanwhile, combine 3/4 cup of the sour cream and flour and whisk until blended. Whisk the mixture into the beets. Keep the soup hot over low heat.

• Beat the egg yolk together with the remaining sour cream and divide it among 4 soup bowls. Ladle the soup into each bowl, and stir to combine it with the egg-yolk mixture. Sprinkle with the croutons.

Per serving: 164 calories, 16g carbohydrates, 4g protein, 10g fat

PREP TIME: 15 MINUTES   COOKING TIME: 15 MINUTES

Onion Soup Cobbler

MAKES 8 SERVINGS

Here's a topping for French onion soup that won't burn your mouth the way that traditional soaked piece of cheese-topped bread does. This tender bumpy or "cobbled" biscuit crust is made with cornmeal and flavored with pesto.

8 cups French onion soup, homemade, canned, or
  from a dried mix
4 cups beef broth

COBBLER TOPPING
1/2 cup all-purpose flour
1/2 teaspoon baking powder
1/4 teaspoon baking soda
1/4 teaspoon salt
1/3 cup cornmeal or fine semolina
1/3 cup plain yogurt
1 large egg, beaten
1 tablespoon melted butter
2 tablespoons pesto sauce
1/4 cup grated Parmesan cheese

• Preheat the oven to 400 degrees. Heat the soup and broth until hot and ladle it into 8 ovenproof serving bowls or large custard cups. Place the bowls on a sturdy baking sheet.

• Combine the flour, baking powder, baking soda, and salt in a large bowl. Stir in the cornmeal and set aside.

• In a smaller bowl, whisk together the yogurt, egg, and melted butter and quickly whisk with the flour mixture. Fold in the pesto, leaving the pesto in streaks. (Do not overmix.)

• Drop the cobbler mixture by spoonfuls over the soup in each bowl, leaving the mounds to give a "cobbled" effect. Sprinkle with the Parmesan cheese.

• Bake the soup on the baking sheet for easy handling until the topping has risen and is golden brown, 10 to 15 minutes.

Per serving: 176 calories, 20g carbohydrates, 9g protein, 7g fat

PREP TIME: 10 MINUTES   COOKING TIME: NONE

Cold Avocado, Spinach & Green Onion Soup

MAKES 6 SERVINGS

The walkways of heaven will probably be lined with avocado trees. Here's a soup to enjoy until then.

2 large ripe avocados

1 lime

4 green onions

1 (5-ounce) bag ready-to-use baby spinach

2 1/2 cups chilled chicken or vegetable broth; more
   if needed

a few drops Tabasco

dash of Worcestershire sauce

salt and pepper to taste

ice cubes if desired

FOR SERVING (OPTIONAL)

lightly toasted French bread

Boursin or other cream cheese

- Halve, pit, peel, and coarsely chop the avocados. Place in a bowl and squeeze the juice from the lime over them. Toss to coat. Snip the scallions into short segments into the same bowl.

- Reserve a few spinach leaves for garnish. Combine the remainder with the avocado mixture and, in batches, purée in a food processor. Scrape out the purée into a bowl and whisk in enough broth to get a runny but thick consistency. Season to taste with Tabasco and Worcestershire sauce, salt, and pepper.

- Pour the soup into individual bowls, adding a few ice cubes if you like. Snip slivers of the reserved spinach leaves on top for garnish.

- Serve with toasted French bread spread with Boursin or other cream cheese.

Per serving (without the bread and cheese): 106 calories, 6g carbohydrates, 4g protein, 8g fat

QUICK COOKS' TIP:

If you opt to serve a cheese or spread infused with green onions, such as scallions or chives, you will find that the depth of flavor in the soup is quite enhanced.

Pea & Cilantro Soup

MAKES 6 SERVINGS

This soup can be served hot or cold.

2 ounces butter
1 large onion, finely chopped
2 garlic cloves, peeled and chopped
1 green chile, seeded and finely chopped
1 pound fresh or frozen peas
8 cups chicken broth
2 tablespoons chopped fresh cilantro
salt to taste
freshly ground pepper to taste
pinch of sugar

GARNISH
softly whipped cream
fresh cilantro leaves

- Melt the butter in a large stockpot over medium heat and add the onion, garlic, and chile and cook, stirring, for 3 to 4 minutes. Add the peas and the broth. Heat to boiling and simmer for 7 to 8 minutes. Add the cilantro.

- Cool the soup until it stops steaming and, in batches, purée in a blender, pouring each batch into a clean saucepan to rewarm if serving hot or into a bowl if serving cold.

- Season the soup with salt, pepper, and a pinch of sugar. Reheat or chill the soup as desired. Serve with a swirl of whipped cream and a few cilantro leaves.

Per serving: 258 calories, 15g carbohydrates, 11g protein, 17g fat

QUICK COOKS' TIP:

Fresh peas are abundant and sweetest in the spring and summertime, but frozen peas really give you delicious results and are ready in a snap.

PREP TIME: 10 MINUTES   COOKING TIME: 45 MINUTES

Spinach & Tangerine Soup

MAKES 8 SERVINGS

7¹/2 cups chicken broth

7 1/2 cups chicken broth

1/2 cup yellow split peas, soaked

1 ounce unsalted butter

3/4 cup sliced scallions

1 teaspoon turmeric

*8 ounces spinach, cleaned, trimmed, and finely
   chopped*

1 cup loosely packed parsley leaves, chopped

*1 cup loosely packed fresh cilantro leaves, chopped,
   plus sprigs for garnish*

grated rind and juice of 2 tangerines

grated rind of 1 orange

2 tablespoons ground rice

1 cup plain yogurt, sour cream, or crème fraîche

• Heat the chicken broth to boiling in a 3-quart saucepan. Add the split peas and simmer for 10 minutes. Melt butter in a small skillet over medium heat and sauté the scallions until softened, about 5 minutes. Add the turmeric and sauté until fragrant, about 1 minute. Stir the scallion mixture into the broth and peas and rinse out the skillet with some broth.

• Add the spinach, parsley, cilantro, grated citrus rind, and tangerine juice to the soup. Cover the pan and simmer for 30 minutes.

• Mix the ground rice with 5 ounces cold water in a cup until blended and stir into the soup. Simmer 15 minutes longer, stirring occasionally.

• Serve in bowls with a little yogurt and fresh cilantro sprigs.

Per serving: 128 calories, 13g carbohydrates, 9g protein, 5g fat

PREP TIME: 5 MINUTES   COOKING TIME: 17 MINUTES

Egg Drop Soup

MAKES 4 SERVINGS

Bouillon cubes make a flavorful and quick broth, but you may need to use low-sodium soy sauce or 4 cubes to 6 cups water to obtain the optimum saltiness. Taste as you go.

1 tablespoon peanut oil or vegetable oil

1/2 cup finely chopped celery

1/4 cup finely chopped onion

6 cups chicken broth or vegetable stock

1 tablespoon soy sauce

2 teaspoons rice wine

1/4 teaspoon white pepper or more to taste

3 egg whites

2 green onions, minced

2 tablespoons mixed cilantro leaves and
    chopped roots

salt to taste if necessary

● Heat oil in a 2-quart saucepan over medium heat and add celery and onion. Sauté 7 minutes, until tender. Add broth, soy sauce, wine, and pepper and heat to boiling. Simmer over low heat 10 minutes.

● Lightly beat egg whites until frothy in a bowl with chopsticks and slowly pour into soup. Do not stir or the soup will get cloudy. Let stand 1 minute, until egg whites set. Add green onions and cilantro and heat through for 1 minute. Taste and adjust seasoning if necessary. Ladle into bowls.

Per serving: 118 calories, 4.5 g carbohydrate, 11g protein, 6g fat

Mushroom Soup with Tomato-Garlic Bruschetta

MAKES 2 SERVINGS

1 tablespoon butter

1 teaspoon vegetable oil

6 ounces mushrooms, chopped, plus a few wafer-thin
  slices for garnish

a pinch of freshly ground pepper

2 teaspoons all-purpose flour

1¼ cups chicken broth

½ cup half-and-half or milk

1 tablespoon heavy cream for garnish

a few leaves of fresh basil, shredded

Tomato-Garlic Bruschetta for serving (recipe follows)

• Melt the butter in the oil in a 2-quart saucepan and sauté the chopped mushrooms with a pinch of pepper. Sauté until the mushrooms are softened, about 4 minutes. Stir in the flour until blended. Mix in the broth and heat to boiling, stirring. Simmer until the soup thickens, about 5 minutes.

• Using a hand blender, purée the mushrooms into the liquid. Stir in the half-and-half and heat through. When hot, serve quickly with a swirl of cream over the top and a sprinkling of raw mushroom slices and basil. Serve with the Tomato-Garlic Bruschetta.

Per serving (without the Bruschetta): 182 calories, 9g carbohydrates, 8g protein, 13g fat

Tomato-Garlic Bruschetta

MAKES 16 SERVINGS

1 dash olive oil

1 tablespoon finely chopped onion

1 (8-ounce) can chopped tomatoes

1 teaspoon tomato paste

1 teaspoon finely chopped garlic

1 pinch fennel seeds (optional)

1 small (8-inch) loaf French bread

• Heat the oil in a small nonstick skillet over medium heat and sauté the onion until tender, about 5 minutes. Stir in the tomatoes, tomato paste, garlic, and fennel seeds, if using. Cook gently until thickened, about 5 minutes.

• Slice the bread diagonally into ½-inch-thick pieces. Toast on both sides. Spread one side of each slice with the tomato mixture and serve immediately.

Per serving: 50 calories, 9g carbohydrates, 2g protein, trace fat

Escarole Soup with Turkey Meatballs

MAKES 6 SERVINGS

1 pound ground turkey

2 eggs, lightly beaten

1 garlic clove, minced

1 small onion, minced

1/2 cup dried breadcrumbs

1/2 cup freshly grated Parmesan cheese

1/2 cup chopped fresh parsley

1 1/2 teaspoons salt

1/4 teaspoon freshly-ground black pepper

3 tablespoons olive oil

1/2 head escarole leaves, washed well and chopped
   (about 1 quart)

1 1/2 quarts canned low-sodium chicken broth or
   homemade broth

2 tablespoons red- or white-wine vinegar

1/4 teaspoon crushed red-pepper flakes

● In a medium bowl, mix together the turkey, eggs, garlic, onion, breadcrumbs, Parmesan, parsley, 1/2 teaspoon of the salt, and the black pepper until thoroughly combined. Shape the mixture into 20 meatballs.

● In a large skillet, heat 1 1/2 tablespoons of the oil over medium heat. Add half the meatballs to the pan and cook, turning, until browned on all sides, about 3 minutes. Remove the meatballs from the pan and drain on paper towels. Repeat with the remaining 1 1/2 tablespoons of oil and the rest of the meatballs.

● Place all the meatballs, the escarole, broth, 2 cups water, the vinegar, red-pepper flakes, and the remaining 1 teaspoon of salt in a large pot. Cover and bring to a simmer over medium heat, stirring occasionally. The meatballs should be cooked through by the time the broth comes to a simmer.

Per serving: 323 calories, 11g carbohydrates, 26g protein, 19g fat

Spicy Corn Chowder

MAKES 6 TO 8 SERVINGS

1/4 cup chopped pancetta or slab bacon

1/4 cup chopped red onion

1/2 teaspoon crushed red pepper flakes

2 cups chopped cauliflower

1 cup canned creamed corn

1 cup 1/2-inch pieces fresh green beans

4 cups vegetable broth or chicken broth

1 cup heavy cream

salt and freshly ground pepper to taste

CHIPOTLE CREAM

1 tablespoon chipotles in adobo, chopped, or
   1 teaspoon crushed dried chipotles

1/2 cup crème fraîche

2 tablespoons snipped fresh chives

• Cook bacon, onion, and pepper flakes in 3-quart saucepan over medium-high heat until onion is tender, about 3 minutes. Add vegetables, broth, and cream and heat to boiling. Simmer 5 to 10 minutes.

• While soup cooks, make Chipotle Cream: Whisk chipotles with crème fraîche and chives.

• To serve: Taste soup and season. Serve in bowls with a dollop of Chipotle Cream.

Each of 8 servings: 249 calories, 10g carbohydrates, 5g protein, 22g fat

Cold Plum Soup with Blue Cheese & Radicchio

MAKES 6 SERVINGS

1 (8-ounce) can plums packed in water, undrained

1 cup red wine

2 cups plain yogurt

1/2 teaspoon cinnamon

1/4 teaspoon ground cloves

1/4 cup fresh lime juice

2 cups cold sparkling water

freshly grated nutmeg to taste

1 cup finely shredded radicchio

1/4 cup crumbled blue cheese

• Purée plums with their liquid in a food processor. Set aside.

• Whisk together yogurt with lime juice, cinnamon, and cloves in a large glass measure until blended. Add plum mixture and the sparkling water. Season with nutmeg. Ladle into bowls; sprinkle with radicchio and blue cheese.

Per serving: 106 calories, 10g carbohydrates, 5g protein, 3g fat

PREP TIME: 10 MINUTES COOKING TIME: NONE

Cuban Avocado Soup

MAKES 6 SERVINGS

2 ripe avocados, pitted and peeled

Juice of 1 lime or more to taste

2 cups plain low-fat yogurt

3 cups vegetable broth or chicken broth

4 fresh basil leaves, torn

pinch of cayenne pepper

salt and freshly ground pepper to taste

• Dice avocados in large chunks; place in food processor with lime juice and yogurt. Pulse until blended; process until smooth. Scrape into a 2-quart bowl or plastic food-storage container; whisk in broth. Stir in basil. Season with cayenne, salt, and pepper. Cover; refrigerate until serving.

Per serving: 153 calories, 10g carbohydrates, 8g protein, 10g fat

PREP TIME: 8 MINUTES COOKING TIME: 5 MINUTES

Asian Crab Soup

MAKES 6 SERVINGS

2 tablespoons vegetable oil

4 green onions, trimmed and chopped

1 cup crabmeat

6 cups fish stock or chicken broth

2 tablespoons rice wine or dry sherry

1 teaspoon grated peeled fresh ginger

1/4 teaspoon freshly ground pepper

salt to taste

2 egg whites, slightly beaten

2 tablespoons minced ham

1 tablespoon chopped fresh cilantro

• Heat oil in 3-quart saucepan and add green onions. Sauté 2 minutes, until softened and fragrant. Add crab, stock, wine, ginger, pepper, and salt. Heat to boiling. Gradually whisk in egg whites, using chopsticks to separate whites into strands as they cook. Heat 1 minute, until whites are firm but not tough.

• Serve in small bowls. Sprinkle each with a little bit of ham and cilantro.

Per serving: 188 calories, 3 g carbohydrate, 18g protein, 11g fat

PREP TIME: 10 MINUTES   COOKING TIME: 15 MINUTES

Fish Soup with Spicy Red Pepper Sauce

MAKES 6 TO 8 SERVINGS

Rouille is the name for this traditional Provençal red pepper sauce, which is served with soups. This version has the lovely smoky flavor of chipotles.

SPICY RED PEPPER SAUCE:

1 (7-ounce) jar roasted red peppers

1 egg yolk

2 tablespoons red-wine vinegar

1 teaspoon chipotles in adobo sauce or more to taste

2 garlic cloves, crushed through a press

1/2 cup olive oil

juice of 1/2 lemon or more to taste

FOR THE SOUP:

1 tablespoon olive oil

1 bulb fennel, stems discarded, chopped
   (reserve fern)

1/2 teaspoon saffron threads

4 cups fish stock or chicken broth

1 (16-ounce) can stewed tomatoes

juice and grated zest of 1 orange

1 teaspoon dried thyme leaves

8 ounces scrod or snapper fillet, cut into
   1/2-inch pieces

8 ounces shelled, deveined shrimp

8 ounces lump crabmeat, picked over

salt and freshly ground pepper to taste

● Make sauce: Combine peppers, egg yolk, vinegar, garlic, 1 teaspoon chipotles, and salt in food processor; purée. With machine running, pour in oil in a slow, steady stream until emulsified. Season with lemon juice and more chipotles, if desired. Set aside.

● Make soup: Heat oil in 3-quart saucepan over medium-high heat. Add fennel and sauté 2 minutes. Add saffron and broth and heat to boiling. Add tomatoes, orange juice, and zest. Reduce heat to medium-low and simmer 10 minutes, stirring occasionally.

● Increase heat to medium-high. When mixture boils, add fish and shrimp; cover and cook 2 minutes, until shrimp are pink. Stir in crab and heat through. Remove from heat. Taste and adjust seasonings. Season with Spicy Red Pepper Sauce.

Each of 8 servings: 282 calories, 10g carbohydrates, 20g protein, 18g fat

QUICK COOKS' TIP:

The rouille makes a great topping for grilled fish steaks as well as a cocktail sauce substitute for shrimp.

Vegetarian Hot & Sour Soup

MAKES 4 SERVINGS

Most hot and sour soups available at Chinese food restaurants these days are made with a pork base. Here is a delicious meatless version.

1 (4-inch) square fresh tender (but not silken) tofu
salt
3 cups vegetable broth
8 ounces sliced mushrooms
2 tablespoons cider vinegar
1 tablespoon soy sauce
1/2 teaspoon white pepper
1/4 cup water
1 1/2 tablespoons cornstarch
1 egg
1 teaspoon dark sesame oil
2 thin green onions, trimmed and chopped

• Gently cut tofu into 2 x 1/4-inch strips. Sprinkle with salt; set aside.

• Heat broth, mushrooms, vinegar, soy sauce, and pepper in 2-quart saucepan to boiling over medium-high heat. Blend water and cornstarch; stir into soup and keep stirring until boiling, thickened, and clear. Gently add tofu.

• Beat egg in bowl; remove pan from heat; slowly pour in egg. Let stand a few seconds; stir gently to swirl cooked egg through soup in strands. Drizzle with oil and sprinkle with onions.

Per serving: 111 calories, 8g carbohydrates, 9g protein, 5g fat

Salads

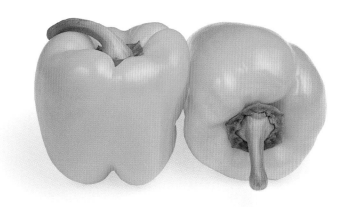

PREP TIME: 10 MINUTES   COOKING TIME: 30 SECONDS

Four-Onion Slaw

MAKES 8 SERVINGS

2 tablespoons nigella seeds (also called onion seeds)

1 cup plain yogurt

1/2 cup sour cream

2 tablespoons fresh lemon juice

2 green onions, trimmed and very finely sliced

1 small sweet onion, sliced into paper-thin rings

1 small red onion, sliced into paper-thin rings

1 fennel bulb, thinly sliced

2 cups cole slaw mix (shredded green cabbage, red
    cabbage, and carrots)

salt and freshly ground pepper to taste

• Dry-fry the nigella seeds in a small skillet over medium-high heat until fragrant, about 30 seconds, and place in a large bowl. Add the yogurt, sour cream, and lemon juice; whisk until smooth. Add onions, fennel, and cole slaw; stir until coated. Season with salt and pepper.

Per serving: 67 calories, 8g carbohydrates, 3g protein, 3g fat

PREP TIME: 10 MINUTES   COOKING TIME: NONE

Blood Orange and Fennel Slaw

MAKES 4 SERVINGS

1 large fennel bulb

2 blood oranges

2 tablespoons fresh lemon juice

2 tablespoons extra-virgin olive oil

salt and freshly ground pepper to taste

4 ounces hard grating cheese such as aged Monterey
    Jack, Gouda, Pecorino, Asiago, or Parmigiano-
    Reggiano

1/4 cup pomegranate seeds or chopped fresh or dried
    cranberries or cherries

2 tablespoons torn or shredded basil or mint leaves

• Trim fennel and cut into thin shreds with a knife or mandoline. Place in bowl. Peel oranges over the same bowl and cut out segments over bowl to catch all juices. Add lemon juice and oil; toss to coat. Season with salt and pepper. Spoon onto salad plates; shave cheese in long, thick shreds on top. Sprinkle with pomegranate seeds and herbs.

Per serving: 148 calories, 10g carbohydrates, 11g protein, 8g fat

PREP TIME: 10 MINUTES   COOKING TIME: NONE

Radicchiously Easy Slaw

MAKES 4 SERVINGS

DRESSING:

3 tablespoons balsamic vinegar

2 tablespoons olive oil

1 teaspoon honey mustard

salt and freshly ground pepper to taste

2 heads radicchio, shredded

1/2 cup crumbled blue cheese

1/4 cup coarsely chopped walnuts, lightly toasted

• Mix dressing ingredients in a large bowl. Add radicchio and cheese; toss to mix and coat. Sprinkle with walnuts.

Per serving: 206 calories, 4g carbohydrates, 5g protein, 20g fat

PREP TIME: 10 MINUTES   COOKING TIME: NONE

Salmon Sashimi Salad

MAKES 4 SERVINGS

8 ounces sliced smoked salmon, cut into thin strips

1 cup thinly sliced celery

1 cup thinly sliced red radishes or daikon

4 perfect leaves of Boston or Bibb lettuce

DRESSING

1 tablespoon dry sherry

1 tablespoon soy sauce

pinch of salt

1 green onion, finely chopped

1 teaspoon dark sesame oil

• Mix dressing in medium bowl. Add salmon, celery, and radishes; toss to coat. Place lettuce leaves on plates; fill with salad.

Per serving: 94 calories, 3g carbohydrates, 11g protein, 4g fat

Crispy Bacon & Avocado Salad

MAKES 6 SERVINGS

This color- and texture-rich salad makes a delicious light supper or lunchtime dish or an accompaniment for a picnic or barbecue. Use bottled balsamic dressing for convenience, or whip up a batch from your favorite recipe.

4 ounces thick-slice bacon
1 tablespoon olive oil
2 slices bread, cubed
1 garlic clove, crushed
12 cups mixed salad greens
4 ounces cherry tomatoes, halved
1 ripe avocado, pitted, peeled, and sliced
12 black olives, halved and pitted
1 yellow pepper, seeded and diced
4 hard-cooked eggs, shelled and quartered lengthwise
1/3 cup bottled balsamic vinaigrette dressing

● Fry the bacon in a skillet until crisp, drain on paper towels, and cut into cubes. Clean the skillet, add the oil, and place over medium heat. Add the bread cubes and garlic and cook until the croutons are golden, 2 to 3 minutes. Drain well on paper towels.

● Arrange the salad greens, tomatoes, avocado slices, olives, and diced pepper on a large serving platter. Sprinkle the bacon and croutons over the salad. Arrange the eggs on top. Drizzle with the vinaigrette just before serving.

Per serving: 333 calories, 13 g carbohydrate, 9g protein, 28g fat

PREP TIME: 10 MINUTES   COOKING TIME: NONE

Juicy Summer Salad

MAKES 6 SERVINGS

How do you put the "crunch" into ripe melon? Use jicama! This amazing root vegetable is a staple in Mexican cuisine and is celebrated for its juicy and crunchy qualities. Its consistency is similar to a cross between a potato and an apple.

1/2 medium jicama, peeled and cut in julienne strips
1/2 medium cantaloupe, cut into 1/2 -inch cubes
2 tablespoons chopped fresh mint
1 teaspoon grated lime rind
3 tablespoons lime juice
1 teaspoon honey
1/4 teaspoon salt

• Combine the jicama, melon, mint, lime rind and juice, honey, and salt in a glass or plastic bowl. Toss to coat.

Per serving: 43 calories, 10g carbohydrates, 1g protein, trace fat

QUICK COOKS' TIP:

Jicama has a thick skin; therefore the best way to peel this vegetable is by first cutting off the root ends crosswise. That way you have a stable base from which to work. Then simply slice the dark skin from top to bottom, moving around the vegetable so that you are left with the white tasty flesh.

PREP TIME: 10 MINUTES   COOKING TIME: NONE

Arugula and Parmigiano Salad

MAKES 4 SERVINGS

4 cups packed cleaned arugula leaves (2 bunches)
1/2 cup extra-virgin olive oil
1 tablespoon grated lemon zest
2 tablespoons fresh lemon juice, or more to taste
salt to taste
8 ounces sliced porcini mushrooms
1 pound Parmigiano-Reggiano cheese, in one chunk

• Place arugula in large bowl. Drizzle with 1/4 cup oil; sprinkle with lemon zest and juice and salt. Toss to coat. Taste and add more lemon juice if needed.

• With a cheese plane, shave off large, thin pieces of cheese and place on plates to form a base, using most but not all of the cheese. (It's easier to remove nice pieces from a large piece.) Top with mushrooms and drizzle with remaining oil. Top with arugula mixture.

Per serving: 595 calories, 6g carbohydrates, 33g protein, 49g fat

PREP TIME: 15 MINUTES   COOKING TIME: NONE

Vegetable Salad Niçoise

MAKES 4 SERVINGS

For anchovyphobes, use julienned carrots or red and/or green bell peppers to make the lattice.

1/2 pound green beans, trimmed, cooked, cooled

1 English cucumber, peeled, thinly sliced crosswise

1 cup cherry tomatoes, halved

1 (2-ounce) jar anchovy fillets, drained, sliced lengthwise into long slivers

32 halves pitted, oil-cured black olives

1/4 cup Dijon Vinaigrette (recipe follows)

● In shallow serving dish, place green beans. Cover with a thin layer of cucumber slices. Make a lattice of anchovies on top, and fill in each space with an olive half. Arrange tomatoes around edge. Sprinkle with dressing and serve.

Per serving: 67 calories, 6 g carbohydrate, 3g protein, 4g fat

PREP TIME: 5 MINUTES   COOKING TIME: NONE

Dijon Vinaigrette

MAKES 1 CUP

This is a tasty blend to use on salads and for marinading.

2 garlic cloves, crushed

1 cup loosely packed Italian parsley leaves

1/3 cup vegetable oil or olive oil

1/4 cup fresh lemon juice

1/4 cup red-wine vinegar

2 tablespoons Dijon mustard

1 teaspoon salt

1 teaspoon grated lemon zest

1/2 teaspoon freshly ground pepper

Whisk together all ingredients until smooth.

QUICK COOKS' TIP:

For a more substantial salad, sprinkle 2 cups of diced firm tofu or diced, cooked chicken and a couple of chopped hard-cooked eggs over the bottom of the dish before adding the vegetables.

PREP TIME: 15 MINUTES   COOKING TIME: NONE   MARINATING TIME: 30 MINUTES

Slivered Cucumber & Chicken Salad

MAKES 2 SERVINGS

Because of the simplicity of the salad, it is important to use juicy chicken.

3 to 4 Kirby cucumbers, *peeled and julienned*

1 large cooked chicken breast half, *skinned, boned, and julienned*

DRESSING

2 tablespoons rice vinegar

1 tablespoon soy sauce

1/2 teaspoon dry yellow mustard or dry wasabi

1/2 teaspoon salt

1 teaspoon toasted sesame seeds for serving

• Combine cucumbers and chicken in a bowl. Mix dressing ingredients in a cup and drizzle on top. Toss to coat. Cover and marinate in refrigerator 30 minutes to 1 hour. Serve cold, sprinkled with sesame seeds.

Per serving: 150 calories, 4g carbohydrate, 28g protein, 2g fat

QUICK COOKS' TIP:

The best method for preparing the juiciest chicken is to poach the breast most of the way and let it finish cooking in its poaching liquid.

BLT Salad

MAKES 4 SERVINGS

The flavors of the perfect BLT sandwich are here in breadless form.

8 cups torn romaine lettuce leaves
1/4 pound slab bacon, diced into
*   1/2 -inch pieces*
1 tablespoon olive oil
1 pint cherry tomatoes, halved
1 clove garlic, crushed through a press
1/2 teaspoon freshly ground pepper
2 tablespoons red-wine vinegar

• Place lettuce in salad bowl. Cook bacon in large skillet until crisp; remove to bowl. Discard all but 1 tablespoon fat from pan. Add olive oil; heat over medium-high heat. Add tomatoes; sauté 1 minute. Add garlic and pepper; sauté 30 seconds. Add vinegar; stir to coat. Pour over lettuce; toss to coat.

Per serving: 200 calories, 6g carbohydrate, 8g protein, 17g fat

Steak Caesar Salad

MAKES 4 SERVINGS

1 teaspoon garlic salt
1/2 teaspoon freshly ground pepper
1 tablespoon anise-flavored liqueur
1 tablespoon soy sauce
1 tablespoon olive oil
1 pound flank steak (in one piece)
1 (16-ounce) bag washed, torn romaine lettuce
1/2 cup bottled Caesar salad dressing
1/4 cup prepared croutons or dry seasoned stuffing mix
2 tablespoons freshly grated Parmigiano-Reggiano
*   cheese*

• Mix garlic salt, pepper, liqueur, soy sauce, and olive oil in medium nonstick skillet. Add steak; turn to coat. Cook 5 minutes on each side over medium-high heat (for medium-rare); remove to cutting board.

• Place romaine in large bowl; toss with dressing, croutons, and cheese. Place on plates. Cut steak into thin slices across the grain; arrange over salad.

Per serving: 307 calories, 6g carbohydrates, 26g protein, 19g fat

PREP TIME: 30 MINUTES (10 MINUTES IF USING PRECUT VEGETABLES)   COOKING TIME: NONE
STANDING TIME: 30 MINUTES (OPTIONAL)

Chopped Salad

MAKES 6 SERVINGS

This is a tasty mix of favorite ingredients in proportions that look good and add the right amounts of juice and crunch.

1/2 *English cucumber, seeded and cubed*

6 *cherry tomatoes, quartered*

2 *ounces button mushrooms, quartered*

1 *cup finely shredded red cabbage*

1 *cup finely shredded green cabbage*

1 *cup small cauliflower florets*

1 *cup baby carrots, peeled and thinly sliced*

1/2 *cup unsalted peanuts*

1/2 *cup chickpeas, cooked; or canned, drained,*
   and rinsed

2 *tablespoons sunflower or olive oil*

1 *tablespoon fresh lemon juice*

salt to taste

freshly ground pepper to taste

3/4 *cup grated cheddar cheese*

• Combine the prepared vegetables in a large salad bowl and toss to mix. Add the peanuts and chickpeas and toss again.

• Whisk the oil and lemon juice together in a small bowl, add the salt and pepper to taste, and whisk again. drizzle the dressing over the salad and leave to stand up to 30 minutes for the flavors to develop.

• Sprinkle the cheese over the salad before serving.

Per serving: 213 calories, 12g carbohydrates, 9g protein, 15g fat

QUICK COOKS' TIP:

If you are on your way home from work craving the freshness of a salad, but have no time to chop, you can buy most produce already trimmed, sliced, and packaged in small portions. Some grocery stores even have in-house salad bars you can raid.

Hearts of Palm & Prosciutto Salad

MAKES 6 SERVINGS

4 ounces arugula salad mix

1 (14-ounce) can hearts of palm, drained, cut into 1/2-inch slices

1 cup diced cantaloupe

6 ounces thinly sliced prosciutto di Parma or other ham, cut into 2-inch pieces

1/4 cup olive oil

2 tablespoons white-wine vinegar

1 teaspoon grated lemon zest

1 teaspoon grainy mustard

pinch each salt and freshly ground pepper

• Combine salad mix, hearts of palm, melon, and ham in salad bowl. Combine remaining ingredients in a jar with a tight-fitting lid; shake to blend. Drizzle salad with dressing; toss.

Per serving: 169 calories, 8g carbohydrates, 7g protein, 13g fat

Cheese, Tomato & Cucumber Salad

MAKES 4 SERVINGS

1 to 2 tablespoons red-wine vinegar

1 teaspoon chopped fresh thyme

1 teaspoon Dijon mustard

1/4 cup olive oil

salt and freshly ground pepper to taste

1 English cucumber, halved lengthwise, seeded with a spoon, and diced into 1/2-inch pieces

2 green onions, trimmed and chopped

1 cup chopped plum or halved grape tomatoes

2 cups coarsely shredded aged Balkan sheep's milk cheese, kasseri, or ricotta

• Whisk 1 tablespoon vinegar, the thyme, and mustard in a large bowl. Whisk in oil gradually until blended. Season with salt, pepper, and more vinegar if needed.

• Add cucumber, onions, and tomatoes to dressing; toss to coat. Spoon into 4 deep soup bowls. Sprinkle each with cheese. Cover and refrigerate until serving.

Per serving: 340 calories, 7g carbohydrates, 12g protein, 30g fat

PREP TIME: 5 MINUTES   COOKING TIME: 15 MINUTES

Warm Poached Egg, French Bean & Tomato Salad

MAKES 4 SERVINGS

2 small garlic cloves, crushed

1/4 cup crème fraîche

2 tablespoons red-wine vinegar

2 teaspoons Dijon mustard

salt and freshly ground pepper to taste

2 (10-ounce) packages frozen French beans

4 plum tomatoes

4 eggs

extra-virgin olive oil for drizzling

• Mix garlic, crème fraîche, vinegar, and mustard in a medium bowl; season with salt and pepper. Add a little hot water if needed to make dressing a thin coating consistency.

• Cook beans as package label directs; drain, add to dressing, and toss to coat. Cut tomatoes in half lengthwise; remove seeds using your thumb. Slice tomatoes lengthwise into strips; add to bowl with beans. Toss to coat with dressing. Spoon onto large plates.

• When ready to serve, bring a deep oiled skillet of salted water to simmering. Crack eggs in separate custard cups or ramekins. Swirl water gently with a wooden spoon and slide one egg at a time into the center of the swirl. This motion will set the yolk and whites perfectly. When slightly set, repeat with remaining eggs.

• When eggs are cooked to desired doneness, remove to paper-towel-lined plate with a slotted spoon. Pat tops gently with paper towel. Trim off strands of white to make eggs look neat. Place an egg on top of each salad; drizzle oil around edge of salads.

Per serving: 178 calories, 10g carbohydrates, 9g protein, 12g fat

PREP TIME: 5 MINUTES   COOKING TIME: 5 MINUTES

Stir-Fried Watercress Salad

MAKES 4 SERVINGS

2 *bunches watercress, trimmed, rinsed, and spun dry*

1 *tablespoon soy sauce*

1 *tablespoon rice vinegar*

1/4 *teaspoon salt*

1/4 *teaspoon sugar*

1 *tablespoon vegetable oil*

1 *garlic clove, crushed through a press*

1/4 *teaspoon crushed red-pepper flakes*

2 *teaspoons dark sesame oil*

2 *teaspoons sesame seeds*

● Chop watercress into rough 2-inch pieces on cutting board; set aside. Mix soy sauce, vinegar, salt, and sugar in ramekin until salt and sugar dissolve; set aside.

● Heat oil in wok over high heat. Add garlic and pepper flakes; stir-fry until fragrant, 1 minute. Add watercress; stir-fry 1 minute. Pour soy-sauce mixture around edges of pan (don't just dump it in the middle.) Stir-fry until watercress is tender, about 3 minutes.

● Place salad in serving bowl. Drizzle with oil; toss to coat. Sprinkle with sesame seeds.

Per serving: 71 calories, 2g carbohydrates, 2g protein, 7g fat

Vietnamese Pork Salad in Rice-Paper Wraps

MAKES 4 SERVINGS

12-ounce pork tenderloin

1/4 cup roasted garlic teriyaki sauce

2 1/2 cups prepared cole slaw mix (shredded green
    and red cabbage and carrots)

1/4 cup mint leaves (no stems)

1/4 cup tender cilantro sprigs

5 tablespoons Vietnamese fish sauce or Thai fish
    sauce (nuoc mam or nam pla)

5 tablespoons fresh lime juice

crushed red pepper flakes

4 (8-inch) rice-paper rounds

1 star fruit (carambola), cut into 8 thin stars

• Cut tenderloin crosswise into 1/4-inch thick slices. Stack 4 slices and cut into 1/4-inch wide strips. Repeat with remaining slices. Place pork and teriyaki sauce in large nonstick skillet; mix well. Cover and steam over medium-high heat 4 minutes. Stir; cover and steam until pork is cooked through, about 2 minutes longer.

• Remove pork to bowl using a slotted spoon. Add cole slaw mix, mint, cilantro, and 1 tablespoon each fish sauce and lime juice. Toss to mix. Mix remaining fish sauce and lime juice and a pinch of pepper flakes in a small bowl; pour into 4 small dishes to use for dipping.

• Fill a shallow dish with warm water. Place a clean kitchen towel on counter next to dish. Submerge a rice-paper round into water; let stand until soaked, about 15 seconds. Place on towel. Repeat with remaining rice-paper rounds.

• Place one-fourth of salad on the bottom third of each round. Fold up bottom edge to cover salad. Tuck in the 2 sides; roll up to make a cylinder. Cut in half on the diagonal; tuck a star fruit slice in the open end of each. Place 2 halves on each of 4 plates. Serve with bowls of dipping sauce.

Per serving: 148 calories, 10g carbohydrates, 20g protein, 3g fat

Eggs & Cheese

Vegetable Egg Foo-Yong •
Tomato Seafood Frittata •
Roasted Vegetable Frittata •
Corn and Shrimp Omelet •
Persian Omelet •
Baked Western Omelets •
Spicy Scrambled Eggs •
Egg and Cheese Wraps •
Confetti Eggs with Asparagus •
and Smoked Salmon

• Spanish-Style Eggs Cooked with
Peppers & Tomatoes
• Midnight Supper Eggs
• Eggs with Spicy Onion Sauce
• Baked Eggs with Spinach and Cheese
• Bacon-Cheese Melt
• Deviled Eggs
• Minute Steaks and Eggs
• Crusty Fried Mozzarella
• Grilled Goat-Cheese Boats

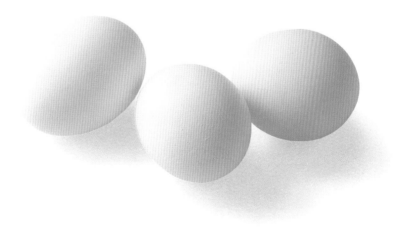

PREP TIME: 10 MINUTES   COOKING TIME: 10 MINUTES

Vegetable Egg Foo-Yong

MAKES 4 SERVINGS

1/4 cup vegetable broth or water

1 small red bell pepper, sliced

8 ounces fresh bean sprouts

1/2 cup chopped celery

1/4 cup chopped green onions

2 tablespoons roasted garlic teriyaki sauce

8 eggs

1/2 teaspoon salt

2 tablespoons peanut or vegetable oil

1 teaspoon cornstarch

• Heat broth to boiling in 10-inch nonstick skillet over medium-high heat. Add vegetables and teriyaki sauce; cover and cook until vegetables are crisp and tender, about 3 minutes. Pour into a strainer placed over a bowl.

• Beat eggs with salt in bowl. Dry out skillet with paper towel. Add oil; heat thoroughly. Add eggs; cook without stirring, lifting eggs at edges as they cook, allowing uncooked portion to slide underneath. When eggs are firm but still wet, spread vegetables over top. Fold one half of the omelet over the other; cover and cook 1 minute. Slide onto warm platter. Keep warm.

• Mix cornstarch with drained broth mixture until blended. Pour into skillet; stir until boiling and thickened, about 1 minute. Pour over eggs.

Per serving: 248 calories, 8g carbohydrates, 8g protein, 15g fat

PREP TIME: 30 MINUTES   COOKING TIME: 25 MINUTES

Tomato Seafood Frittata

MAKES 8 SERVINGS

One man's omelet is another man's scrambled eggs. But both the Italians and the Spaniards make a sturdy, portable egg cake that can sit around awhile in a picnic basket while a bottle of white wine chills in a cold stream. But fresh out of the oven, this rich tomato-red mixture of vegetables, shrimp, squid, and crabmeat will not get as far as the dining-room table. A salad with a tangy lemon vinaigrette is all that is needed.

1 small white onion, unpeeled, left whole, plus 1
    medium white onion, finely chopped

2 garlic cloves, unpeeled

5 bay leaves

1 1/2 to 2 teaspoons salt

1 pound unshelled shrimp

1/2 pound cleaned squid, diced

1 pound lump crabmeat, picked over

1 pound tomatoes, peeled, seeded, and chopped

1/4 cup chopped flat-leaf parsley

2 jalapeño peppers, seeded and finely chopped

2 tablespoons flour

4 eggs, separated

1 tablespoon olive oil

- Combine the whole onion, garlic, bay leaves, 1 teaspoon salt, and 2 quarts water in a stockpot or large saucepan. Heat to boiling over high heat, then reduce the heat and simmer 5 minutes. Add the shrimp and cook 3 minutes, skimming off any froth.

- Remove the shrimp with a slotted spoon, drain well, transfer to bowl, and set aside to cool. Remove and discard the onion and garlic from the stockpot, add the squid, and cook 3 minutes. Remove squid from the pot, drain, and set aside. Reserve the seafood broth for another purpose (it makes delicious fish soup).

- When the shrimp are cool enough to handle, peel, devein, and finely chop them. Combine the shrimp, squid, crabmeat, chopped onion, tomatoes, parsley ,and peppers in a large bowl and mix well. Sprinkle

with the flour and $1/2$ to 1 teaspoon more salt and toss again until no flour can be seen.

- Beat the egg whites in bowl until slightly stiff peaks form. Beat the egg yolks, one at a time, into the seafood mixture until thoroughly incorporated. With a rubber spatula, carefully fold in the egg whites.

- Heat the oil in a skillet over medium-high heat until hot and fragrant. Reduce the heat to low. Pour or spoon seafood mixture into pan, smoothing it with spatula to spread it evenly down to the bottom of pan. Cook uncovered 8 minutes. Flip the cake by sliding onto pan lid or plate and slipping it back into pan. Cook until golden on underside, about 3 minutes. Serve hot, cut into wedges.

Per serving: 216 calories, 8g carbohydrate, 31g protein, 6g fat

Roasted Vegetable Frittata

MAKES 4 SERVINGS

12 ounces sliced Portobello mushroom caps

6 thin green onions, trimmed, cut into 1-inch lengths

1/2 cup roasted red peppers (homemade or
    store-bought)

2 tablespoons extra-virgin olive oil

2 garlic cloves, crushed through a press

1 teaspoon dried Italian herb seasoning mix or
    oregano

1 teaspoon salt

1/2 teaspoon freshly ground pepper

8 eggs

1 cup shredded provolone or Asiago cheese

2 tablespoons milk or water

3 tablespoons butter

• Preheat broiler. Line broiler pan with foil. Spread out mushrooms, onions, and peppers in pan. Mix garlic with oil, Italian seasoning, 1/2 teaspoon salt, and 1/4 teaspoon pepper; drizzle over vegetables; toss to coat. Broil 6 inches from heat 5 to 7 minutes, stirring every 3 minutes. Set aside. Keep broiler on.

• Beat eggs, remaining salt and pepper, and the cheese and milk in a bowl. Melt butter over medium-high heat in 10-inch skillet with ovenproof handle; add eggs. Cook without stirring until eggs set in a thin layer. Cook, lifting frittata at edges to allow uncooked eggs to slide underneath.

• While there is still a good layer of uncooked eggs, sprinkle evenly with vegetable mixture. Broil until set, about 3 minutes. Loosen frittata with thin metal spatula without scraping pan. Slide or flip frittata out onto a warm platter. Serve hot or at room temperature, cut into wedges.

Per serving: 378 calories, 9g carbohydrates, 24g protein, 28g fat

Corn and Shrimp Omelet

MAKES 4 SERVINGS

1 pound shelled shrimp, finely chopped

3 garlic cloves, crushed through a press

2 green onions, trimmed, chopped

1/2 cup yellow corn kernels (fresh, frozen, or canned)

1/4 cup chopped red bell pepper

1 1/2 tablespoons cornstarch

1 tablespoon nuoc mam or nam pla
   (Vietnamese/Thai fish sauce)

1/2 teaspoon freshly ground pepper

4 eggs

2 tablespoons vegetable oil

● Place shrimp, garlic, onions, corn, pepper, cornstarch, nuoc mam and pepper in medium bowl; mix very, very well. Add eggs; stir until shrimp mixture is coated; do not overmix.

● Heat oil in large (10-inch) nonstick skillet over medium-high heat until hot but not smoking. Add shrimp mixture, spreading lightly to cover pan bottom. Reduce heat to medium; cover loosely with lid. Let cook 3 minutes, until edges of omelet start to come away from pan. Lift omelet (if it isn't set, increase heat slightly and cook another 1 to 2 minutes before lifting) and spread uncooked portion to edges. Cover, leaving lid slightly ajar; cook until set on top and browned on bottom, about 5 minutes.

● Invert omelet onto baking sheet; slide back into skillet. Cook, mostly covered with lid, until browned on bottom side, about 4 minutes. Invert or slide onto baking sheet and transfer to heated serving plate. Cut into wedges or squares. Serve hot or warm.

Per serving: 293 calories, 10g carbohydrates, 30g protein, 14g fat

PREP TIME: 5 MINUTES   COOKING TIME: 25 MINUTES

Persian Omelet

MAKES 3 SERVINGS

Garnish this dazzling green-flecked golden dish with watercress that has been drizzled with herb oil and tossed to coat. The juicy, peppery cress not only tastes wonderful with the eggs, but also adds a fresh aroma to the fragrance that rises from the cooked herbs and saffron.

softened butter for greasing the baking dish

6 eggs

2 tablespoons clarified butter

2 scallions, trimmed and chopped

1 cup loosely packed fresh cilantro leaves, chopped

1 cup loosely packed fresh flat-leaf parsley leaves, chopped

1/4 cup finely snipped fresh chives

1 tablespoon finely snipped fresh dill

1/4 teaspoon saffron threads, crumbled

salt to taste

freshly ground pepper to taste

For Serving

1 small bunch young, tender watercress, rinsed, dried, and trimmed

Basil Oil (recipe follows)

6 tablespoons plain yogurt

• Preheat the oven to 350 degrees. Grease a shallow 1 1/2-quart baking dish with butter.

• Lightly whisk the eggs in a large bowl and add the clarified butter, scallions, herbs, saffron, salt, and pepper. Whisk until well blended. Pour the mixture into the prepared dish and bake until set but still very moist, 20 to 25 minutes.

• Meanwhile, in a medium bowl, mix the watercress with a drizzle of Basil Oil. Toss to coat.

• To serve: Cut the omelet into wedges and place a wedge on each serving dish. Garnish with the watercress and serve with yogurt.

Per serving: 400 calories, 7 g carbohydrate, 16g protein, 35g fat

PREP TIME: 5 MINUTES   COOKING TIME: NONE

Basil Oil

MAKES 1/2 CUP

1/4 cup loosely packed fresh basil leaves

1/2 cup olive oil

salt to taste

freshly ground pepper to taste

● Combine the basil and oil in a blender and season with salt and pepper. Purée until the oil is finely flecked with the basil.

Per serving: 120 calories, trace carbohydrates, 0g protein, 14g fat

PREP TIME: 10 MINUTES   COOKING TIME: 10 MINUTES

Baked Western Omelets

MAKES 4 SERVINGS

butter for greasing dishes

6 eggs

2 tablespoons water

2 teaspoons roasted garlic teriyaki sauce or soy sauce

1 tablespoon vegetable oil

1 small red bell pepper, chopped

1 small green bell pepper, chopped

1 small red onion, chopped

1 (3-ounce) square firm tofu, drained, patted dry and diced into 1/2-inch pieces

1 cup shredded Monterey Jack cheese with jalapeños

● Preheat oven to 450 degrees. Butter 4 (6-ounce) ramekins; place on rimmed baking sheet. Beat eggs with water and teriyaki sauce in large bowl; set aside.

● Heat oil thoroughly in medium nonstick skillet over medium-high heat. Add vegetables and tofu; sauté until tender, about 3 minutes. Pour into egg mixture; stir in cheese and mix well. Spoon into prepared ramekins. Bake until firm but not dry, 5 to 6 minutes. Serve dishes on small hot mats on plates.

Per serving: 299 calories, 6g carbohydrates, 19g protein, 23g fat

Spicy Scrambled Eggs

MAKES 2 TO 3 SERVINGS

A lifelong carnivore, I spontaneously went vegetarian when I traveled through Nepal and India. Eggs popped up in some of the most interesting and delicious dishes I've ever eaten. This is a representative sample.

6 *large eggs*

1/4 teaspoon salt

1/8 teaspoon freshly ground pepper

pinch of ground turmeric

3 tablespoons clarified butter

1 large onion, finely chopped

1 garlic clove, crushed through a press

1 jalapeño pepper, finely chopped

1 teaspoon grated, peeled fresh ginger

1 small tomato, peeled, seeded, and finely chopped

3 tablespoons finely chopped fresh cilantro

● Lightly beat eggs in a bowl with salt, pepper, and turmeric. Heat butter in a nonstick skillet over medium heat until hot; sauté onion, garlic, jalapeño, and ginger 5 minutes, until softened and fragrant. Add tomato; sauté 1 minute. Stir in eggs; cook, stirring frequently until egg is just set. Sprinkle with cilantro and serve.

Each of 3 servings: 276 calories; 7g carbohydrates, 14g protein, 22g fat

PREP TIME: 10 MINUTES   COOKING TIME: 10 MINUTES

Egg and Cheese Wraps

MAKES 4 SERVINGS

4 (8-inch) rice-paper rounds

6 eggs, beaten

2 tablespoons water

1/4 teaspoon salt

1 tablespoon vegetable oil

1 small red bell pepper, chopped

1 small onion, chopped

4 tablespoons shredded sharp cheddar cheese

4 tablespoons salsa

• Fill a shallow dish with warm water. Place a clean kitchen towel on counter next to dish. Submerge a rice-paper round into water; let stand until soaked, about 15 seconds. Place on towel. Repeat with remaining rice-paper rounds.

• Beat eggs with water and salt in large bowl. Set aside.

Heat oil in medium nonstick skillet over medium-high heat. Add vegetables and sauté until tender, about 3 minutes. Pour in eggs; cook, stirring, until eggs are set.

• Place one-fourth of eggs on the bottom third of each rice-paper round. Sprinkle with cheese and salsa. Fold up bottom edge to cover salad. Tuck in the 2 sides; roll up to make a cylinder. Cut in half on the diagonal.

Per serving: 197 calories, 7g carbohydrates, 12g protein, 14g fat

Confetti Eggs with Asparagus and Smoked Salmon

MAKES 4 SERVINGS

6 egg whites

4 whole eggs

1/2 teaspoon freshly ground pepper

1/4 cup snipped fresh dill

4 ounces smoked salmon, cut into thin strips

1 tablespoon butter

1 tablespoon olive oil

1 bunch (1 pound) asparagus, trimmed, cut into
    1/4-inch pieces

1 small red bell pepper, chopped

4 ounces sliced mushrooms, chopped

1/2 cup chopped celery

• Whisk egg whites, eggs, dill, and pepper in large bowl until blended. Stir in salmon; set aside.

• Melt butter in oil in 10-inch nonstick skillet over medium-high heat. Add vegetables; sauté until tender, about 5 minutes. Add eggs; stir until ingredients are evenly distributed. Scramble occasionally until eggs are set.

Per serving: 233 calories, 10g carbohydrates, 21g protein, 13g fat

Spanish-Style Eggs Cooked with Peppers & Tomatoes

MAKES 4 SERVINGS

An abundance of vegetables makes a nest for these eggs as they cook. Serve at once with crusty garlic bread.

2 tablespoons olive oil

3 large red and/or green bell peppers, stemmed,
*   seeded, and sliced*

1 large onion, sliced

2 large tomatoes, chopped

1 tablespoon Pesto Sauce (recipe follows)

salt to taste

freshly ground pepper to taste

4 large eggs

12 black olives, pitted and chopped

1 tablespoon shredded fresh basil leaves

• Heat the oil in a large skillet over medium heat and gently fry the peppers and onion until colored and softened, about 8 minutes. Stir in the tomatoes and Pesto and season well. Using two wooden spoons, make 4 wells in the vegetable mixture in the pan and crack an egg into each. Sprinkle the eggs with salt, black pepper, olives, and basil.

• Reduce heat and cover the pan, cooking for a further 3 to 5 minutes, depending how well done you like your eggs.

Per serving: 301 calories, 17g carbohydrate, 10g protein, 23g fat

Pesto Sauce

MAKES ABOUT 3/4 CUP

2 garlic cloves, crushed

2 large bunches fresh basil leaves, torn up

1 tablespoon pine nuts

a pinch of salt

3 1/2 ounces olive oil

2 tablespoons freshly grated Parmesan cheese

2 tablespoons freshly grated pecorino cheese

• Combine the garlic, basil leaves, pine nuts, and a little salt in a food processor and purée. With the machine running, slowly pour in the olive oil. Scrape out the mixture into a bowl and stir in the cheeses.

• To make the pesto the old-fashioned way, combine the garlic, basil leaves, pine nuts, and a little salt in a mortar and pound with a pestle to a paste. Slowly pour in the olive oil as you keep pounding and add the cheeses.

Per tablespoon: 90 calories, 1g carbohydrates, 1g protein, 9g fat

Midnight Supper Eggs

MAKES 4 SERVINGS

8 large eggs

1/3 cup heavy cream

4 tablespoons unsalted butter, cut into small pieces

1/4 teaspoon salt

1/4 teaspoon freshly ground pepper

• Place all ingredients into a medium stainless-steel mixing bowl. Place over a pan of simmering water. Make sure pan does not touch water.

• Whisk all ingredients continuously until eggs are semi-set in small soft curds, about 10 minutes.

Per serving: 277 calories, 2g carbohydrates, 13g protein, 24g fat

PREP TIME: 10 MINUTES COOKING TIME: 25 MINUTES

Eggs with Spicy Onion Sauce

MAKES 4 SERVINGS

2 tablespoons ground coriander

1 teaspoon fennel seeds, ground in a spice mill or mortar

1/2 teaspoon ground cumin

1/4 teaspoon turmeric

1/8 teaspoon cayenne pepper

1/8 teaspoon freshly ground pepper

1/8 teaspoon cinnamon

1/8 teaspoon ground cloves

1/8 teaspoon ground cardamom

1/3 cup water

3 tablespoons vegetable oil

1/2 teaspoon mustard seeds

10 curry leaves or 2 bay leaves

1 dried red chile

2 medium onions, thinly sliced

1 teaspoon salt

1 cup chopped tomatoes

1/4 cup canned unsweetened coconut milk

8 extra-large eggs, hard-cooked and peeled

● In a bowl, combine the coriander, fennel, cumin, turmeric, cayenne, black pepper, cinnamon, cloves, and cardamom with 1/3 cup of water to make a paste.

● In a large nonstick skillet, warm the oil over medium high heat and add the mustard seeds. When they begin to pop, add the curry leaves and dried red chile and cover. After most of the seeds have popped, uncover, add the onions, and cook, stirring occasionally, until softened and lightly browned, about 6 minutes.

● Add the spice paste and salt and cook over medium heat for 5 minutes, adding a few tablespoons of water if the pan is dry. Add the tomatoes and 3/4 cup of water and simmer over low heat, stirring occasionally, until the tomatoes are soft and the sauce is thick. Add the coconut milk and eggs, spooning the sauce over the eggs. Heat to simmering, cover, and cook over low heat until the eggs are heated through. Serve at once.

Per serving: 298 calories, 9 g carbohydrate, 14g protein, 24g fat

Baked Eggs with Spinach and Cheese

MAKES 4 SERVINGS

butter for greasing dishes
1 cup frozen chopped spinach, thawed
1/4 cup heavy cream
4 eggs
4 thin (but not paper thin) slices prosciutto di
   Parma or other ham such as Serrano
1/4 cup shredded yellow cheddar cheese
salt and freshly ground pepper

• Preheat oven to 450 degrees. Butter 4 shallow baking dishes such as crème brulée dishes or ramekins; place on rimmed baking sheet.

• Spoon spinach into dishes; drizzle with cream. Break an egg into center of each dish. Place ham and cheese around egg; sprinkle lightly with salt and pepper. Bake until eggs are set to desired doneness, 6 to 8 minutes. Serve dishes on small hot mats on plates.

Per serving: 231 calories, 3g carbohydrates, 13g protein, 19g fat

Bacon-Cheese Melt

MAKES 6 SERVINGS

This makes a nice hot open-face sandwich and a dip for raw vegetables.

1 (8-ounce) package cream cheese, softened
1/4 cup (2-percent fat) milk, or more if needed
1 tablespoon Dijon mustard
2 cups (8 ounces) shredded cheddar cheese
4 ounces bacon, cooked until crisp and crumbled
2-inch chunks of celery for dipping

• Place cream cheese, milk, and mustard in medium microwave-safe bowl. Cover with plastic wrap; microwave 2 to 3 minutes, until cream cheese is softened. Stir until smooth. Stir in cheese until blended. Microwave 2 to 3 minute or until cheese is melted, stirring every minute. Thin with more milk if needed. Stir in bacon.

Per serving: 331 calories, 3g carbohydrates, 15g protein, 29g fat

QUICK COOKS' TIP:

This topping also works on grilled tofu and flounder, and for steamed vegetables.

Deviled Eggs

MAKES 4 TO 6 SERVINGS

The recipes that endure are the ones that touch our hearts as well as our stomachs. This is a modestly glamorized version of what is considered to be the best basic deviled egg.

6 large eggs (if you want to be fancy, use 12 quail
  eggs; cook only 5 minutes)
1 (8-ounce) package cream cheese, softened
1/2 teaspoon curry powder
1/4 teaspoon dry mustard
1/4 cup chopped almonds, toasted
2 tablespoons finely chopped candied ginger, cut
  into small pieces

● Place eggs in a pan large enough to hold them in a single layer; cover with cold water. Heat to boiling over medium-high heat, cover, turn off the heat, and let eggs sit 15 minutes. Drain and run under cold water until eggs are completely cool.

● Peel eggs and cut in half lengthwise. Place yolks in bowl. Add cream cheese, curry powder, and mustard; beat until smooth. Cover; refrigerate several hours so flavors can blend. Let spread stand at room temperature about 30 minutes before serving to soften.

● To serve: Place curry mixture in pastry bag fitted with large star tip; pipe into centers of egg whites. Mix almonds and ginger in a cup; sprinkle over eggs.

Each of 6 servings: 244 calories; 3.5g carbohydrates, 20g protein, 21g fat

PREP TIME: 10 MINUTES   COOKING TIME: 10 MINUTES

Minute Steaks and Eggs

MAKES 4 SERVINGS

5 eggs

1 tablespoon soy sauce

1/4 cup rice flour

1 teaspoon lemon-pepper seasoning

1/4 teaspoon garlic powder

3 tablespoons butter

1 tablespoon vegetable oil

1 1/2 pounds minute steaks

2 tablespoons water

2 tablespoons freshly snipped chives (optional)

• Preheat oven to 300 degrees. Beat 1 egg with the soy sauce in a shallow bowl. Mix flour, pepper seasoning, and garlic powder in another shallow bowl. Coat one steak with egg mixture; drain off excess. Coat with flour mixture; shake off excess. Place on plate. Repeat with remaining steaks.

• Melt 1 tablespoon butter in oil in large nonstick frying pan over medium-high heat. Add steaks; brown 2 minutes on both sides. Place on oven-safe platter; cover loosely with foil. Keep steaks warm while frying eggs.

• Wipe out skillet; melt remaining butter over medium-high heat. Add remaining eggs, one at a time. Add 2 tablespoons water. Cover; reduce heat to medium. Cook eggs to desired doneness, 2 to 3 minutes. Sprinkle with chives; serve with steaks.

Per Serving: 413 calories, 9g carbohydrates, 37g protein, 24g fat

Crusty Fried Mozzarella

MAKES 8 SERVINGS

1/4 cup flour or all-purpose flour

1 egg

2 tablespoons water

3/4 cup fine dried Italian bread crumbs

1/4 teaspoon garlic salt

8 ounces mozzarella, cut into 8 (1/2-inch-thick)
   slices

vegetable oil for frying

• Place flour on a plate. Beat egg with water in a shallow bowl. Mix breadcrumbs and garlic salt on another plate.

• Dredge cheese slices in flour; shake off excess. Coat with egg; drain off excess. Coat completely with crumbs.

• Heat 2 inches oil until hot but not smoking in deep large skillet over medium-high heat. Using long-handled tongs, place slices into oil (do not crowd) and fry until golden, turning once, about 2 minutes in all. Drain on paper towels.

Per serving: 152 calories, 10g carbohydrates, 8g protein, 9g fat

Grilled Goat-Cheese Boats

MAKES 4 SERVINGS

2 medium zucchini, cut in half lengthwise

1 tablespoon olive oil

1 garlic clove, crushed through a press

4 marinated sun-dried tomatoes, slivered

12 ounces fresh goat cheese

3 tablespoons dried Italian-seasoned breadcrumbs

2 tablespoons slivered fresh basil

4 small sprigs fresh basil

• Preheat broiler. Line broiler pan with foil.

• Scoop out zucchini insides with a grapefruit spoon; reserve insides. Place zucchini boats in prepared pan; brush with oil. Broil 6 inches from heat source until slightly softened, about 3 minutes. Set aside. Keep broiler on.

• Finely chop scooped-out portion of zucchini. Heat oil in medium nonstick skillet over medium-high heat; add chopped zucchini and garlic; sauté 2 minutes.

• Remove pan from heat. Stir in tomatoes, cheese, breadcrumbs, and slivered basil; mix well. Spoon into zucchini boats; broil until heated through, about 4 minutes. Garnish with basil sprigs.

Per serving: 371 calories, 10g carbohydrates, 20g protein, 29g fat

Meat

Gorgonzola Cheeseburgers on Crostini •

Pan-Fried Steaks and Stroganoff Sauce •

Filet Steaks with Herb Butter •

Garlic-Glazed Flank Steak •

Sautéed Beef with Stout •

Broiled Steak au Poivre to Order •

Curried Beef & Potatoes •

Stir-Fried Ginger and Brandy Beef •

Spicy Orange Beef with Broccoli •

Skillet Salsa Beef •

Pan-Grilled Liver with Sherry Onion Sauce •

Veal Chops Milanese •

Parma Veal •

• Ground Lamb Kebabs with Yogurt-Dill Sauce

• Quick Lamb Cassoulet

• Stir-Fried Sesame Lamb

• Spiced Broiled Lamb Chops

• Thai Pork Chops

• Balsamic Grilled Smoked Pork Chops

• Grilled Pork Medallions with Pineapple Sauce

• Stir-Fried Pork with Baby Leeks

• Pan-Fried Venison Steaks with Bourbon Butter Sauce

• Hot Muffuletta

PREP TIME: 10 MINUTES COOKING TIME: 10 MINUTES

Gorgonzola Cheeseburgers on Crostini

MAKES 4 SERVINGS

A fabulous modern spin on a classic food!

8 ounces ground sirloin or chuck

salt to taste

freshly ground pepper to taste

8 thin slices pancetta

4 ounces Gorgonzola cheese cut into 4 (3/4-inch-
   thick) slices

4 slices Italian bread

1 large garlic clove, sliced in half

8 basil leaves, shredded

1/2 cup chopped tomato

1/4 cup chopped red onion

extra-virgin olive oil for drizzling

- Preheat the broiler or prepare an outdoor grill for barbecuing. Shape the meat into 4 patties and season on both sides with salt and pepper. Wrap each hamburger in 2 slices of pancetta.

- Broil the burgers about 5 inches from the heat source or grill the burgers over a medium-hot fire for about 4 minutes, or until the pancetta is nicely browned. Flip the burgers and top them with the Gorgonzola. Grill for about 4 minutes longer, or until nicely browned on the second side and cooked through.

- Meanwhile, rub the cut sides of the garlic over the bread and grill the bread on both sides until lightly toasted. Combine the basil, tomato, and onion in a small bowl and sprinkle with salt and pepper. Toss to mix.

- To serve: Place one crostini on a serving plate. Top with the basil mixture and drizzle with oil. Set the burgers on top and serve at once.

Per serving: 485 calories, 13g carbohydrates, 24g protein, 31g fat

PREP TIME: 5 MINUTES   COOKING TIME: 15 MINUTES

Pan-Fried Steaks and Stroganoff Sauce

MAKES 4 SERVINGS

These steaks are so fast yet so good. A unique blend of spices gives them an extra kick!

4 (8-ounce) boneless steaks (sirloin, rib-eye, tender-loin), 1/2-inch thick

1 tablespoon oil

kosher salt

freshly ground pepper

8 ounces sliced mushrooms

1 tablespoon butter

2 shallots, finely chopped

4 sprigs fresh thyme

2 tablespoons brandy

1 cup sour cream

1 teaspoon Dijon mustard

• Heat a large heavy nonstick or cast-iron skillet over medium-high heat until smoking. Rub steaks on both sides with oil, then salt and pepper. Fry steaks 2 to 3 minutes on both sides (for medium-rare) and remove with tongs to warm plate. Cover and keep warm.

• Add mushrooms to drippings in pan; sauté until tender, about 2 minutes. Remove to plate with steaks. Melt butter in pan; add shallots and thyme; sauté until shallots are tender, 1 minute. Add brandy and boil until reduced by half.

• Remove thyme stems. Whisk sour cream and mustard into shallots. Stir in mushrooms and any steak drippings on plate. Stir until heated through. Pour over steaks.

Per serving: 510 calories, 6g carbohydrates, 41g protein, 34g fat

Filet Steaks with Herb Butter

MAKES 4 SERVINGS

Herb butter is the perfect accent for a good piece of meat.

1 cup red wine
1 cup low-sodium beef broth
2 cups parsley leaves
1 cup watercress leaves
1/2 cup 1-inch lengths snipped fresh chives
8 tablespoons butter, softened
1 garlic clove, crushed through a press
salt to taste
freshly ground pepper to taste
4 (6-ounce) beef filet steaks

• Preheat broiler. Combine wine and broth in small saucepan; heat to boiling over medium-high heat. Boil until reduced by half, about 10 minutes.

• Meanwhile, heat small saucepan of water to boiling. Add parsley, watercress, and chives; boil until wilted, 30 seconds. Drain through sieve; rinse in cold water until cool. Pat dry with paper towels; place in food processor. Add butter, garlic, salt, and pepper; process until blended. Set aside.

• Line broiler pan with foil; place rack on top. Place steaks on rack; season on both sides with salt and pepper. Smear top side with some of the butter mixture. Broil 4 inches from heat 4 minutes; turn and smear top side with more butter mixture. Broil 4 minutes longer for medium-rare. Place on warm platter.

• Whisk the remaining butter mixture, a little dollop at a time, into wine mixture over medium heat. (Do not boil or sauce will separate.) When sauce is smooth, taste; adjust seasoning if needed. Serve with steaks.

Per Serving: 551 calories, 4g carbohydrates, 38g protein, 36g fat

PREP TIME: 5 MINUTES   COOKING TIME: 8 MINUTES

Garlic-Glazed Flank Steak

MAKES 4 SERVINGS

You and your family will be left wondering, how could something so easy and fast taste so good?

1-pound flank steak

1/4 cup roasted-garlic teriyaki sauce

2 teaspoons cracked dried green peppercorns

• Preheat broiler; line broiler pan with foil. Score steak with 1-inch diagonal slashes in each direction on both sides.

• Combine sauce and peppercorns in prepared pan; mix well. Place steak in pan; spread sauce on both sides. Broil 4 inches from heat source 4 minutes on each side for medium-rare.

Per Serving: 184 calories, 1.4g carbohydrates, 24g protein, 9g fat

PREP TIME: 15 MINUTES   COOKING TIME: 10 MINUTES

Sautéed Beef with Stout

MAKES 4 SERVINGS

When cooking with alcohol, don't skimp. Rather, use the quality you would drink—it makes all the difference.

2 tablespoons butter

4 large garlic cloves, crushed through a press

1 (1 1/2-pound) boneless sirloin steak, trimmed, cut into 1-inch cubes

1 cup stout or dark beer

2 tablespoons all-purpose flour

1/2 teaspoon Dijon mustard or more to taste

salt and freshly ground pepper to taste

1/4 cup torn fresh parsley leaves

• Melt butter in large skillet over medium-high heat until lightly browned, about 2 minutes. Add garlic and beef; sauté until beef is browned but still rare on the inside, about 5 minutes.

• Combine stout, flour, and mustard in a jar with a tight-fitting lid; shake to blend. Pour into skillet; stir until sauce boils and thickens, about 3 minutes. Season with salt and pepper. Taste and add more mustard if needed. Sprinkle with parsley.

Per Serving: 457 calories, 7g carbohydrates, 34g protein, 30g fat

Broiled Steak au Poivre to Order

MAKES 6 SERVINGS

Extra-thick steaks are so dramatic, and you only have to watch them carefully to make them perfect. You run the risk of cooking them too long on one side so plan to spend the last 5 minutes in front of the broiler to control the surface browning and interior doneness.

1/4 cup red-wine vinegar

1 tablespoon vegetable oil

3 pounds T-bone or porterhouse steak (or steaks),
  as thick as 2 inches

1 teaspoon salt

1 teaspoon freshly ground pepper

1 teaspoon dried basil leaves, crushed

• Preheat the broiler and arrange the oven racks so the surface of the steaks will be 4 inches from the flame or heat element.

• Combine the vinegar and oil in a deep shallow bowl and whisk until blended. Dip the steak or steaks on both sides in the vinegar mixture, drain off the excess, and place on the broiler rack over a broiler pan.

• Combine the salt, pepper, and basil in a small cup. Press half of the mixture onto both sides of the steak or steaks and place on the broiler rack. Broil until the surface is seared and sizzling, about 5 minutes. Turn over the steaks and press the remaining seasoning onto the uncooked side or sides. Cook to the desired degree of doneness, which may mean turning over thick steaks again, cooking 2 or so minutes per side.

Per serving: 319 calories, 0g carbohydrates, 48g protein, 13g fat

Curried Beef & Potatoes

MAKES 4 SERVINGS

It's back to the basics with this recipe: meat and potatoes, but with a very fresh spin!

12 ounces top round beef steak

8 ounces potatoes, peeled, halved, and thinly sliced

1/2 cup beef broth

2 teaspoons cornstarch

1/4 teaspoon salt

nonstick cooking spray

3/4 cup chopped onion

3/4 cup chopped green or red bell pepper

1 tablespoon vegetable oil

1 teaspoon curry powder

1 medium tomato, coarsely chopped

QUICK COOKS' TIP:

Feel free to add leftover cooked vegetables such as carrots, green beans, and squash to the mixture.

- Partially freeze the meat. Thinly slice across the grain into bite-sized strips and set aside.

- Cook the potatoes in boiling water until tender, about 8 minutes. Drain and set aside.

- Combine the beef broth, cornstarch, and salt. Set aside.

- Grease a wok or large skillet with cooking spray. Heat over medium-high heat. Add the onion and stir-fry 2 minutes. Add the bell pepper and stir-fry until the vegetables are crisp and tender, about 2 minutes. Remove to a bowl.

- Add the oil to the hot wok. Add the beef and curry powder. Stir-fry until cooked to the desired doneness, 2 to 3 minutes. Push beef from center of the wok. Stir broth mixture to recombine and add to center of wok. Heat to boiling, stirring until thickened. Stir in onion mixture, potatoes, and tomato. Cook, stirring, until heated through.

Per serving: 209 calories, 17g carbohydrates, 22g protein, 6g fat

PREP TIME: 10 MINUTES   COOKING TIME: 3 MINUTES

Stir-Fried Ginger and Brandy Beef

MAKES 2 SERVINGS

This wonderful combination of flavors is guaranteed to win over your diners!

10 ounces beef, slightly frozen for easier slicing

2-inch piece peeled fresh gingerroot, finely chopped

2 tablespoons brandy

1 1/2 tablespoons soy sauce

1 1/2 tablespoons oyster sauce

1 teaspoon cornstarch

1/2 teaspoon freshly ground pepper

2 tablespoons vegetable oil

2 tablespoons white wine

2 tablespoons beef broth

2 scallions, trimmed and shredded

2 tablespoons chopped fresh cilantro

• Preheat the oven to 200 degrees. Heat an oven-safe serving plate or baking dish.

• Thinly slice the beef and place in a shallow bowl. Add the ginger, brandy, soy sauce, oyster sauce, cornstarch, and pepper, and toss to coat.

• Heat the oil in a wok until smoking. Add the beef and stir-fry 1 minute. Add the wine and broth and stir-fry until the beef is the desired doneness, 1 to 2 minutes longer. Transfer to the hot plate and garnish with scallions and cilantro.

Per serving: 428 calories, 11g carbohydrates, 30g protein, 24g fat

PREP TIME: 5 MINUTES   MARINATING TIME: 10 MINUTES   COOKING TIME: 12 MINUTES

Spicy Orange Beef with Broccoli

MAKES 6 SERVINGS

This recipe adds a little extra flavor to a favorite dish!

1 pound thinly sliced beef top round

1/2 cup chopped green onions

1/4 cup roasted-garlic teriyaki sauce

2 tablespoons grated orange zest

2 tablespoons dry sherry

1 tablespoon rice-wine vinegar

1 tablespoon plus 1 teaspoon cornstarch

4 tablespoons peanut or vegetable oil

1/2 teaspoon crushed red-pepper flakes

2 cups broccoli florets, halved lengthwise if large

1/2 teaspoon salt

1/4 teaspoon sugar

4 tablespoons water

• Cut beef slices into 2-inch-wide strips. Combine beef, onions, sauce, zest, sherry, vinegar, and 1 tablespoon cornstarch in a plastic food-storage bag. Squeeze to mix and coat beef evenly with marinade. Let stand 10 minutes.

• To finish: Heat 2 tablespoons oil in wok over high heat. Add pepper flakes; stir-fry 30 seconds. Add broccoli; stir-fry 2 minutes. Sprinkle with salt and sugar; toss to coat. Add 2 tablespoons water; cover and steam 2 minutes, stirring once. Scrape out into a bowl.

• Heat remaining 2 tablespoons oil in wok over high heat. Add beef and marinade; stir-fry until beef is cooked and browned, 1 to 2 minutes. Add broccoli and juices; stir-fry until hot, 1 to 2 minutes. Mix remaining 1 teaspoon cornstarch with remaining 2 tablespoons water; pour around edges of wok so it goes into liquid. Stir-fry until juices are thickened and shiny, about 2 minutes.

Per Serving: 437 calories, 7g carbohydrates, 33g protein, 30g fat

PREP TIME: 5 MINUTES   COOKING TIME: 10 MINUTES

Skillet Salsa Beef

MAKES 4 SERVINGS

Just because you're eating good carbs doesn't mean you have to miss out. Enjoy this fantastic good-carb spin on tacos!

1 pound flank steak, thinly sliced across the grain
2 tablespoons balsamic vinegar
1 teaspoon dried oregano leaves
1/2 teaspoon garlic powder
5 tablespoons corn oil or other vegetable oil
2 stalks celery, thinly sliced on the diagonal
1 cup hot salsa fresca
2 (8-inch) corn tortillas
1/4 cup tender cilantro sprigs

● Combine beef, vinegar, oregano, and garlic powder in medium bowl; stir to mix.

● Heat 1 tablespoon oil in large nonstick skillet over medium-high heat. Add celery; sauté 1 minute. Add steak mixture; sauté until browned, about 3 minutes. Add salsa; mix well. Cover and simmer 5 minutes.

● While steak mixture cooks, stack tortillas on cutting board and cut with pizza wheel into 1/2-inch wide strips. Heat remaining oil in medium skillet; fry tortilla strips until crisp. Drain on paper towels.

● Spoon steak mixture onto serving dish; sprinkle with tortilla strips and cilantro.

Per Serving: 439 calories, 10g carbohydrates, 32g protein, 30g fat

PREP TIME: 5 MINUTES   COOKING TIME: 15 MINUTES

Pan-Grilled Liver with Sherry Onion Sauce

MAKES 4 SERVINGS

If you're a fan of liver and onions, you'll love this!

4 slices applewood-smoked bacon
4 (4-ounce) slices beef or calves' liver, 1/2-inch thick
salt and freshly ground black pepper
4 medium green onions, trimmed, cut into
   1-inch pieces
1/2 cup dry sherry
salt and freshly ground black pepper

● Fry bacon until crisp in large nonstick skillet over medium-high heat. Drain on paper-towel-lined plate; keep warm.

● Sprinkle liver with salt and black pepper. Fry liver in drippings over medium-high heat until firm and browned on underside, about 3 minutes; turn over and fry until barely cooked through, about 3 minutes. Remove to warm serving platter; cover loosely with foil.

● Add onions to drippings in pan; sauté 1 minute. Add sherry; boil until reduced to 1/4 cup. Season with salt and pepper. Pour over liver; serve each slice topped with a strip of bacon.

Per Serving: 284 calories, 9g carbohydrates, 24g protein, 13g fat

PREP TIME: 10 MINUTES   COOKING TIME: 10 MINUTES

Veal Chops Milanese

MAKES 4 SERVINGS

This classic dish is distinctive because of its cheese coating. The oregano and lemon are not traditional but add nice flavors and aromas.

4 (1-inch thick) veal rib chops, rib bones "frenched"
  by the butcher
1 cup shredded Parmigiano-Reggiano cheese
2 tablespoons fine dried breadcrumbs
1 teaspoon dried oregano leaves
1 teaspoon grated lemon zest
2 eggs
2 tablespoons all-purpose flour
salt and freshly ground pepper
4 tablespoons butter
1/4 cup olive oil
lemon wedges for serving

● Mix cheese, crumbs, oregano, and zest in a shallow dish. Lightly beat eggs in a bowl. Mix flour with 1/2 teaspoon each salt and pepper. Place chops on cutting board; sprinkle on one side with half the mixture and rub it over to coat. Repeat on other side. Brush chops with egg on both sides. Dip in cheese mixture, lightly pressing coating into chops.

● Melt butter in oil in a skillet over medium-high heat. Fry chops until golden on one side, about 3 to 4 minutes; turn the chop and fry the other side until cooked through, 5 to 6 minutes longer. Make sure the oil does not get too hot so the chops do not brown too quickly. Serve with lemon wedges.

Per serving: 557 calories, 7g carbohydrates, 60g protein, 33g fat

Parma Veal

MAKES 4 SERVINGS

This good-carb interpretation of an Italian favorite is so tasty and easy, you will never even think about all the breadcrumbs in the original.

1 egg

1/2 cup freshly grated Parmigiano-Reggiano cheese

2 tablespoons dried Italian-seasoned breadcrumbs

1 1/2 pounds veal scallops

2 tablespoons butter

2 tablespoons olive oil

1/4 cup dry white vermouth

4 thin slices prosciutto di Parma, cut crosswise into
  1/2-inch wide pieces

1/4 cup limoncello (Italian lemon-flavored liqueur)

1 tablespoon torn fresh Italian parsley leaves

2 teaspoons drained small capers

• Beat egg in shallow bowl. Mix cheese and breadcrumbs in another shallow bowl. Coat scallops with egg; drain off excess. Coat with cheese mixture; shake off excess.

• Melt butter in oil in large nonstick skillet over medium-high heat; when butter stops bubbling, fry veal until golden, 1 to 2 minutes. Turn scallops over; fry until golden, 1 to 2 minutes. Remove to warm plate; sprinkle with prosciutto. Cover loosely with foil; keep warm.

• Add limoncello to hot skillet; boil over high heat until syrupy, stirring to clean pan. Stir in parsley and capers; pour over veal.

Per Serving: 515 calories, 3g carbohydrates, 60g protein, 25g fat

PREP TIME: 15 MINUTES COOKING TIME: 10 MINUTES

Ground Lamb Kebabs with Yogurt-Dill Sauce

MAKES 4 SERVINGS

Grill these over charcoal at your next barbecue.

1 *pound ground lamb*
1 *clove garlic, minced*
1 *egg white, lightly beaten*
2 *teaspoons grated lemon zest*
1 *teaspoon ground cumin*
1 *teaspoon onion salt*
1/2 *teaspoon freshly ground pepper*
extra-virgin olive oil for greasing skewers and pan
1 *small onion, thinly sliced*
lemon wedges for serving

YOGURT-CUCUMBER SAUCE

1 *cup plain Greek-style whole-milk yogurt*
1 *Kirby cucumber, halved, seeded, and grated*
1 *large clove garlic, crushed through a press*
1/4 *cup torn fresh mint*
pinch of salt

- Preheat outdoor grill for barbecue or preheat broiler. Combine lamb, garlic, egg white, lemon zest, cumin, onion salt, and pepper in a large bowl; knead with your hand to a paste. Roll into 1-inch-wide, 2-inch-long sausage shapes, wetting hands lightly to keep meat from sticking.

- Wipe 4 long metal kebab skewers with oil, and thread "sausages" through short sides onto skewers, allowing 1/4 inch between pieces and using a dampened hand to gently squeeze meat against the skewers to attach firmly.

- If using a broiler, line broiler pan with foil and brush with oil. Arrange skewers in pan and brush with oil. Grill kebabs 4 inches from heat source, until browned and crisp on all sides, about 10 minutes in all, turning every 2 minutes.

- While kebabs cook, make sauce: Combine ingredients in bowl and mix well.

- Serve with raw onions and lemon wedges.

Per serving: 242 calories, 5g carbohydrates, 15g protein, 18g fat

PREP TIME: 10 MINUTES   COOKING TIME: 40 MINUTES

Quick Lamb Cassoulet

MAKES 8 SERVINGS

A classic cassoulet takes days to assemble and hours to make. This streamlined version is a way to enjoy the essence of the labor-intensive dish without feeling guilty about taking a few shortcuts.

1 tablespoon olive oil

6 slices bacon, coarsely chopped

2 pounds boneless lamb leg steaks, cut into cubes

1 onion, finely chopped

1 garlic clove, crushed

1 carrot, peeled and diced

1 (14-ounce) can chopped tomatoes

3/4 cup red wine

3/4 cup hot lamb or beef broth

1/4 teaspoon dried rosemary, crumbled

1/4 teaspoon thyme leaves, crumbled

1 (14-ounce) can haricot beans, undrained

salt to taste

freshly ground pepper to taste

1 cup chopped fresh parsley

● Heat the oil in a large skillet over medium heat and add the bacon and lamb. Cook until browned, about 10 minutes. Add the onion and garlic and cook until soft, about 5 minutes. Add the carrots and cook, stirring, 2 minutes. Add the tomatoes, wine, broth, and herbs. Cover and cook for 20 minutes until the meat is tender.

● Stir the beans into the cassoulet, heat until bubbly, and season with salt and pepper. Spoon the cassoulet into a heatproof serving dish and sprinkle the parsley on top.

Per serving: 374 calories, 19g carbohydrates, 30g protein, 18g fat

Stir-Fried Sesame Lamb

MAKES 4 SERVINGS

The wonderful marinade and the tasty sauce give this lamb recipe an extra boost.

1 pound boneless lean lamb from the leg or center-cut chops, slightly frozen

MARINADE

2 teaspoons cornstarch

1/2 teaspoon sugar

2 tablespoons soy sauce

1 tablespoon water

1 bunch large green onions

1/4 cup peanut oil

2 garlic cloves, thinly sliced

8 ounces sliced mushrooms

1 (8-ounce) can bamboo shoots, drained and rinsed

2 tablespoons toasted sesame seeds

SAUCE

1 tablespoon soy sauce

1 tablespoon dry sherry

1 tablespoon dark sesame oil

1 teaspoon distilled white vinegar

• Cut lamb into 2- x 1- x 1/8–inch slivers. Place in bowl. Add marinade ingredients; toss with your hands to incorporate marinade into meat. Set aside. Mix sauce ingredients in small bowl; set aside.

• Line up green onions on cutting board with root ends even; trim off root ends in one chop. Trim off dried green portions. With paring knife, quarter each onion lengthwise; line up and cut crosswise into 1-inch pieces.

• Heat wok or large nonstick skillet over high heat. Add oil; when hot but not smoking, add garlic and lamb; stir-fry until lamb pieces are dark brown and firm enough to separate. Add green onions; stir-fry 1 minute. Add mushrooms and bamboo shoots; stir-fry 1 minute.

• Stir sauce and pour around edges of lamb. Stir-fry until sauce thickens and forms a shiny glaze on lamb mixture. Scrape out onto warm platter; sprinkle with sesame seeds.

Per Serving: 370 calories, 10g carbohydrates, 27g protein, 25g fat

Spiced Broiled Lamb Chops

MAKES 4 SERVINGS

Lamb never tasted this good in so little time.

4 (6-ounce) lean lamb rib chops, trimmed

1 garlic clove, crushed through a press

3 tablespoons soy sauce

2 tablespoons hoisin or plum sauce

1 tablespoon vegetable oil

1 teaspoon Chinese 5-spice powder

- Preheat broiler. Line a broiler pan with foil. Place rack in pan; place chops on rack.

- Mix garlic, soy sauce, hoisin, oil, and 5-spice powder in small bowl. Brush on both sides of chops. Broil 3 to 4 inches from heat source for 3 to 4 minutes on each side for medium-rare.

Per Serving: 294 calories, 6g carbohydrates, 27g protein, 17g fat

PREP TIME: 10 MINUTES   COOKING TIME: 15 MINUTES

Thai Pork Chops

MAKES 4 SERVINGS

These juicy, spicy pork chops are easy to coat and quick to cook. There will be seasoning mix left over for your next batch or for cooking chicken or fish.

THAI SEASONING
18 low-sodium sesame-flavored Melba toasts
1 tablespoon garlic powder
1 tablespoon ground ginger
1 teaspoon sugar
1/2 teaspoon cayenne pepper

4 lean center-cut loin pork chops, 1/2-inch thick
1 tablespoon low-sodium soy sauce
nonstick cooking spray

● Place the Melba toasts in a food processor, and process until finely crushed. Combine the crushed Melba toasts and remaining ingredients in a zip-top heavy-duty plastic bag, seal bag, and shake well. Store tightly sealed, shake well before each use. Use as a coating mix for pork or poultry.

● Preheat the oven to 450 degrees. Grease a baking sheet with cooking spray.

● Trim the fat from the pork chops, and brush pork with soy sauce. Place 1/3 cup Thai Seasoning in a large zip-top heavy-duty plastic bag. Add chops, seal bag, and shake to coat. Place chops on the prepared baking sheet and bake until cooked through, about 15 minutes.

Per serving: 283 calories, 12g carbohydrates, 24g protein, 15g fat

PREP TIME: 5 MINUTES   COOKING TIME: 6 MINUTES

Balsamic Grilled Smoked Pork Chops

MAKES 4 SERVINGS

These are perfect alternatives to burgers for your next barbeque!

4 (5-ounce) boneless smoked pork chops

2 cloves garlic, minced

1/4 cup balsamic vinegar

2 teaspoons grated orange zest

2 tablespoons orange juice

1 teaspoon ground cumin

- Prepare outdoor grill for barbecue or preheat broiler. If broiling, line small shallow broiler pan with foil; arrange pork on top.

- Mix remaining ingredients; brush on both sides of pork chops. Broil 4 inches from heat source 2 to 3 minutes on each side, until sizzling and browned.

Per serving: 185 calories, 2g carbohydrates, 25g protein, 8g fat

Grilled Pork Medallions with Pineapple Sauce

MAKES 4 SERVINGS

Pineapples and pork is always a winning combination!

PINEAPPLE SAUCE:

1 (8-ounce) can crushed pineapple in natural juices

1/4 cup cider vinegar

1/4 cup water

1 tablespoon roasted-garlic teriyaki sauce

1 tablespoon cornstarch

Nonstick cooking spray

1 1/2 pounds pork tenderloin, cut crosswise into
    1/2-inch thick medallions

1 tablespoon extra-virgin olive oil

1 tablespoon peanut butter

1 tablespoon honey mustard

1 teaspoon lemon-pepper seasoning

- Make sauce: Combine ingredients in small saucepan; stir until blended. Heat over medium-high heat until boiling and thickened. Keep warm over low heat.

- Preheat broiler. Line broiler pan with foil. Place broiler rack in pan; grease rack with cooking spray.

- Flatten medallions slightly with heel of hand. Place medallions on prepared rack. Broil 4 inches from heat source 2 minutes on each side. While medallions cook, mix oil, peanut butter, mustard, and pepper seasoning in small bowl; brush over medallions. Spread mixture on each side of medallions; broil 1 minute on each side. Serve with sauce.

Per Serving: 299 calories, 10g carbohydrates, 37g protein, 12g fat

Stir-Fried Pork with Baby Leeks

MAKES 4 SERVINGS

Leeks are a wonderful addition to any pork dish. They nicely accentuate the flavor of pork.

1 pound boneless pork shoulder or butt, very
*   thinly sliced*

3 tablespoons roasted-garlic teriyaki sauce

3 tablespoons sweet sherry or mirin (sweet rice wine)

1 tablespoon cornstarch

6 baby leeks or 12 thin green onions

2 tablespoons peanut oil

1 small red bell pepper, thinly sliced

4 ounces snow peas, trimmed

• Combine pork, teriyaki sauce, sherry, and cornstarch in bowl; mix together ingredients using hands to saturate meat with marinade. Set aside.

• Line up leeks on cutting board with root ends even. Cut off root ends; cut crosswise into 1/2-inch pieces.

• Heat wok or large nonstick skillet over high heat. Add 1 tablespoon oil; heat thoroughly. Add vegetables; stir-fry until wilted, 1 minute. Remove to bowl.

• Drain pork mixture, reserving marinade. Heat wok again; add remaining oil and heat until hot. Add pork mixture; stir-fry 3 minutes. Mix marinade; stir into pork. Add vegetables; stir until marinade thickens and glazes mixture.

Per Serving: 408 calories, 10g carbohydrates, 21g protein, 30g fat

PREP TIME: 5 MINUTES   COOKING TIME: 10 MINUTES

Pan-Fried Venison Steaks with Bourbon Butter Sauce

MAKES 4 SERVINGS

4 (1-inch thick) venison steaks, trimmed, patted dry
salt and freshly ground pepper to taste
1 teaspoon allspice berries, crushed in a mortar
6 tablespoons unsalted butter
1 tablespoon olive oil
1/4 cup bourbon
1/2 cup chicken broth
2 tablespoons dried cranberries or other dried fruit

• Season steaks with salt, pepper, and allspice; rub seasonings into meat. In a large heavy skillet over medium-high heat, melt 2 tablespoons butter in oil. Sauté steaks on both sides until browned, 1 to 1½ minutes per side. Remove to a plate, cover, and keep warm.

• Pour bourbon into pan over medium-high heat; stir to loosen any browned bits. Boil until reduced to 1 tablespoon. Add broth and cranberries; simmer until berries plump, about 5 minutes.

• Reduce heat to low; whisk in remaining butter, a little piece at a time, until melted and sauce is thickened. (Do not boil or sauce will "break".) Serve over steaks.

Per Serving: 493 calories, 4g carbohydrates, 43g protein, 25g fat

Hot Muffuletta

MAKES 6 SERVINGS

This sandwich, a New Orleans specialty, is usually served unheated, probably because the weather in The Big Easy is so hot and steamy. In addition to its unconventional melted cheese, this version is made with a crusty baguette. (Try keeping things crisp, even with air conditioning, when the humidity outside is 100 percent!) For more variety, use a combination of chopped, pitted black olives, such as Calamata, and green olives with pimientos in the salad for both color and flavor.

1 (10-ounce) jar green olives with pimientos, drained
  and chopped

1/4 cup chopped fresh parsley

1 1/2 teaspoons dried oregano leaves

1 garlic clove, minced

3 tablespoons olive oil

1 14-inch thin baguette, split, most of the inside
  removed

8 ounces sliced hard salami

8 ounces sliced ham

8 ounces sliced provolone

• Preheat the oven to 350 degrees. In a small bowl, combine the chopped olives with the parsley, oregano, garlic, and oil. Spread some of the olive mixture on the bottom half of the bread.

• Top the olive salad with the salami, ham, and provolone. Cover with the tops of the bread and cut into 6 sandwiches. Wrap each sandwich in aluminum foil. Bake until the cheese melts, about 15 minutes.

Per serving: 513 calories, 20g carbohydrates, 24g protein, 37g fat

Poultry

Steamed Chicken Rolls •
Tamarind Chicken Sates •
Chicken Stuffed with •
Fresh Ginger & Green Onions
Kiwi, Lime & Coconut Chicken •
Sweet and Sour Chicken with Cashews •
Spicy Fried Chicken •
Greek Chicken Sandwiches •

• Crispy Ginger Chicken
• Curried Chicken Stir-Fry with
  Green Beans
• Grilled Turkey & Tomato Burgers
• Stir-Fried Turkey and Vegetables
• Honey Turkey Fajitas
• Turkey Piccata
• Spicy Turkey Lettuce Wraps

PREP TIME: 10 MINUTES   COOKING TIME: 8 MINUTES   COOLING TIME: 5 MINUTES

Steamed Chicken Rolls

MAKES 4 SERVINGS

You won't even miss the crust while enjoying the fabulous flavor of cheese, ham, and arugula in these tasty chicken rolls.

4 (6-ounce) chicken cutlets
smoked Spanish paprika
2 teaspoons finely grated orange zest
kosher salt
4 thin (but not paper-thin) slices Serrano ham
2 cups cleaned arugula
4 ounces thinly sliced Spanish manchego cheese
1/4 cup chicken broth or water

• Prepare a wok or wide steamer with boiling water. Place cutlets apart on work surface; sprinkle with paprika, orange zest, and salt. Top each with ham, a layer of arugula, and then the cheese. Roll up, jelly-roll fashion; secure with wooden picks.

• Place rolls in shallow bowl and cover with broth. Steam in a wok or steamer over boiling water until cheese starts to ooze out, 6 to 8 minutes. (Carefully remove lid to check the progress at 6 minutes.)

• Cool chicken 5 minutes. Cut rolls crosswise at an angle; remove picks and slice. Drizzle with steaming juices. Remove picks; cut rolls into 3 or 4 pieces crosswise at an angle.

Per serving: 230 calories, 2g carbohydrates, 33g protein, 9g fat

PREP TIME: 15 MINUTES   MARINATING TIME: 4 HOURS OR OVERNIGHT   COOKING TIME: 10 MINUTES

Tamarind Chicken Sates

MAKES 4 SERVINGS

The unique tamarind flavor gives this dish an extra oomph.

MARINADE
1/2 cup boiling water
2 tablespoons tamarind paste (available at Indian grocery stores)
2 large garlic cloves, slivered
1/2 cup minced shallots
1/4 cup soy sauce

1 pound chicken cutlets
1 tablespoon coriander seeds, toasted and crushed
salt and pepper to taste
4 green onions, trimmed, cut crosswise into 1-inch pieces

- Pulse boiling water and tamarind in food processor until smooth; add garlic, shallots, and soy sauce. Cut chicken into 1-inch-wide strips; place in bowl. Add marinade; toss to coat. Cover; refrigerate for at least 4 hours or overnight.

- Soak 6-inch wooden skewers in water at least 20 minutes. Prepare outdoor grill for barbecue or preheat broiler. Line broiler pan with foil if using broiler.

- Drain skewers. Thread chicken pieces onto skewers in alternation with onions. Combine coriander with salt and pepper in a shallow bowl. Roll sates in spices. Place sates on grill or in broiler pan. Grill or broil sates on both sides until cooked through, about 10 minutes.

Per serving: 110 calories, 3g carbohydrates, 21g protein, 1g fat

Chicken Stuffed with Fresh Ginger & Green Onions

MAKES 4 SERVINGS

White wine and heavy cream combine to flavor and enrich the sauce. This is great served over a bed of sautéed sugar snap peas.

3 tablespoons olive oil
4 (6-ounce) boneless chicken breasts with the skin on
1 bunch green onions, trimmed and finely chopped
1-inch piece fresh gingerroot, peeled and finely chopped
salt to taste
freshly ground pepper to taste

SAUCE
1/2 cup dry white wine
1/2 cup chicken broth
1/2 cup heavy cream
1-inch piece fresh gingerroot, peeled and thinly sliced
1 bunch green onions, trimmed and finely chopped

• Preheat the oven to 325 degrees. Line a baking pan with aluminum foil.

• Heat 2 tablespoons of the oil in a skillet over a medium-high heat and cook the chicken until just golden brown on the outside but still raw in the center. Remove it to a plate and let cool a little.

• Add another tablespoon of oil to the pan and stir in the scallions and ginger. Gently fry for 5 minutes, until softened but not colored. Remove the pan from the heat and season lightly.

• Using a sharp knife, make 4 oblique cuts, evenly spaced, to the center of each chicken breast. Push a little of the scallion and ginger mixture into each cut so that the flavors penetrate well into the meat. Transfer the chicken to the prepared baking pan and bake 10 to 12 minutes, or until the chicken is cooked through.

• Prepare the sauce: Pour the wine into a small pan and reduce it by half. Add the chicken broth and reduce by half. Stir in the cream, ginger, and green onions. Heat to simmering and season to taste.

• Serve each chicken breast over a bed of sautéed vegetables with the sauce spooned over the top.

Per serving: 638 calories, 16g carbohydrates, 40g protein, 44g fat

Kiwi, Lime & Coconut Chicken

MAKES 4 SERVINGS

This recipe is perfect for a tropical theme party.

4 boneless, skinless chicken breast halves

MARINADE
2 to 3 kiwifruit, peeled and diced
1 tablespoon sherry vinegar
1 tablespoon lime juice
salt to taste
freshly ground pepper to taste

TO COOK CHICKEN
1 ounce butter
1 tablespoon olive oil
1 tablespoon honey

SAUCE
5 ounces canned coconut milk
3 tablespoons heavy cream (optional)
2 kiwifruits, peeled and diced
2 scallions, trimmed and minced
finely grated peel of 1 lime
salt to taste
freshly ground pepper to taste

GARNISH
1 tablespoon finely chopped parsley

● Cut the chicken breasts into generous strips about 1/2 inch thick and 3 inches long.

● Prepare the marinade by mixing together the diced kiwifruit, sherry vinegar, lime juice, and seasonings in a shallow baking dish. Add the chicken strips, toss to coat, and leave to marinate for 30 minutes.

● To cook the chicken, melt the butter in the oil in a large nonstick skillet, add the honey and, when bubbling, add the chicken. The honey will sweeten the chicken during cooking, but be careful not to over-cook. Cook, stirring, for about 5 minutes, until the chicken is almost cooked and the liquid in the pan has reduced.

● Add the coconut milk and, if desired, the cream. Add the diced kiwifruit, scallions, lime peel, salt, and pepper. Simmer gently for 5 to 6 minutes over a low heat until the chicken is cooked through. Cooking time will vary with the thickness of the chicken fillets, but test just before serving. Garnish with finely chopped parsley.

Per serving (with heavy cream): 360 calories, 12g carbohydrates, 29g protein, 23g fat

PREP TIME: 5 MINUTES   MARINATING TIME: 10 MINUTES   COOKING TIME: 6 MINUTES

Sweet and Sour Chicken with Cashews

MAKES 4 SERVINGS

Experience two favorite Chinese dishes in one with this yummy combination of flavor!

1 pound boneless, skinless chicken breasts, cut into 1-inch cubes

3 tablespoons soy sauce

1 1/2 tablespoons sweet Chinese chili sauce

1 tablespoon rice-wine vinegar or distilled white vinegar

2 teaspoons cornstarch

1/4 cup water

2 tablespoons vegetable oil

1/4 cup chopped green onions

1/4 cup chopped celery

1/3 cup salted cashews

• Mix chicken, 1 tablespoon soy sauce, the chili sauce, vinegar, and 1 teaspoon cornstarch in bowl until coated. Let stand 10 minutes.

• For sauce, mix remaining soy sauce and cornstarch with water in a small cup until blended; set aside.

• Heat oil in wok or large nonstick skillet over medium-high heat. Add onions and celery; stir-fry 1 minute. Add chicken mixture; stir-fry 1 to 3 minutes, until chicken is golden-brown. Add cashews; stir-fry 1 minute. Remix sauce; pour around edges of chicken mixture. Stir-fry until sauce boils and thickens into a shiny glaze, about 1 minute.

Per Serving: 439 calories, 10g carbohydrate, 32g protein, 30g fat

PREP TIME: 10 MINUTES   MARINATING TIME: OVERNIGHT   STANDING TIME: 1 HOUR, 5 MINUTES   COOKING TIME: 15 MINUTES

Spicy Fried Chicken

MAKES 4 SERVINGS

You won't miss the flour in this amazing fried chicken recipe.

MARINADE

1 teaspoon cumin seeds

1 teaspoon coriander seeds

1 teaspoon black peppercorns

2 garlic cloves, crushed through a press

2 tablespoons olive oil

1 teaspoon kosher salt

1 teaspoon ground ginger

1/2 teaspoon ground turmeric

1/4 teaspoon ground cinnamon

pinch cayenne pepper

8 boneless chicken thighs (skin on)

2 tablespoons vegetable oil

● Toast cumin and coriander seeds in small skillet over medium heat until fragrant, about 2 minutes. Place in mortar; add peppercorns. Crush; place in bowl. Add garlic, olive oil, salt, ginger, turmeric, cinnamon, and cayenne. Rinse chicken with cold water; pat dry with paper towels. Rub marinade over chicken. Place in glass baking dish; cover. Refrigerate overnight.

● Bring chicken to room temperature, about 1 hour. Heat vegetable oil to shimmering over medium-high heat in deep large skillet. Add chicken; fry, partially covered, until cooked through and crispy on both sides, 10 to 15 minutes, turning after 5 minutes. Let stand 5 minutes; cut crosswise into 1-inch slices.

Per serving: 430 calories, .5g carbohydrates, 33g protein, 32g fat

PREP TIME: 15 MINUTES   MARINATING TIME: 30 MINUTES   COOKING TIME: 12 MINUTES

Greek Chicken Sandwiches

MAKES 4 SERVINGS

Who says hummus is just for vegetables? This great chicken dish proves otherwise.

1/4 cup plain Greek yogurt

2 tablespoons hummus (homemade or store-bought chickpea dip)

1 teaspoon ground cumin

1 teaspoon ground coriander

1/2 teaspoon turmeric

3 tablespoons fresh lime juice

1 tablespoon chopped fresh mint

pinch of salt

4 boneless, skinless chicken breast halves, cut into thin strips

2 tablespoons Basil Oil (recipe follows) for serving

4 white pita bread loaves

mixed salad greens

sliced tomatoes

sliced yellow bell pepper

• Mix together the yogurt and hummus in a bowl, cover, and refrigerate.

• In a shallow bowl blend together the cumin, coriander, turmeric, lime juice, mint, and salt. Add the chicken to the spice mixture, mix well to coat, cover, and leave to marinate in a cool place for at least 30 minutes, stirring occasionally.

• Heat the basil oil in a large skillet over medium heat and fry the chicken until cooked through, 8 to 10 minutes, stirring occasionally, until golden.

• Toast the pita loaves on each side until golden brown. Cut in half crossways, open up, and fill with the chicken mixture. Add salad leaves, tomato slices, and yellow bell pepper slices. Top with a generous spoonful of the hummus-yogurt mixture and serve immediately.

Per serving: 297 calories, 20g carbohydrates, 31g protein, 10g fat

PREP TIME: 5 MINUTES   COOKING TIME: NONE

Basil Oil

MAKES 1/2 CUP

1/4 cup loosely packed fresh basil leaves

1/2 cup olive oil

salt to taste

freshly ground pepper to taste

● Combine the basil and oil in a blender and season with salt and pepper. Purée until the oil is finely flecked with the basil.

Per serving: 120 calories, trace carbohydrates, 0g protein, 14g fat

PREP TIME: 5 MINUTES   COOKING TIME: 15 MINUTES

Crispy Ginger Chicken

MAKES 4 SERVINGS

This zesty recipe puts a great Asian spin on the quintessential American bar food, chicken wings.

8 boneless chicken thighs (skin on)

vegetable oil for frying

1/2 cup rice flour

2 teaspoons ground ginger

1/2 teaspoon garlic salt

lime wedges for serving

● Preheat oven to 300 degrees (optional, if serving immediately). Rinse chicken with cold water; pat dry with paper towels. Heat 1/2 inch oil to shimmering over medium-high heat in deep large skillet.

● Mix flour, ginger, and garlic salt in plastic food storage bag; add thighs, one at a time, and shake to coat. Fry chicken until cooked through and crispy and golden on both sides, 10 to 15 minutes, turning after 5 minutes.

● Drain chicken on paper towels; keep warm in oven or cut crosswise into 1-inch slices (a Chinese cleaver is efficient for whacking off and transferring the slices), and serve immediately with lime wedges.

Per serving: 475 calories, 10g carbohydrates, 33g protein, 32g fat

PREP TIME: 5 MINUTES   COOKING TIME: 10 MINUTES

Curried Chicken Stir-Fry with Green Beans

MAKES 4 SERVINGS

This quick and easy dish should be called curry in a hurry!

2 *tablespoons vegetable oil*

1 *large garlic clove, crushed through a press*

1 *tablespoon curry powder*

1 *tablespoon grated lemon zest*

8 *ounces Chinese long green beans or regular green beans, trimmed, cut into 1-inch pieces*

1 *pound boneless, skinless chicken cutlets, slivered*

1/4 *cup chicken broth or water*

2 *tablespoons fresh lemon juice*

salt to taste

1/2 *cup chopped freshly roasted peanuts*

- Heat 1 tablespoon oil in wok or large nonstick skillet over medium-high heat. Add garlic, curry powder, and zest; stir-fry 30 seconds. Add beans; stir-fry 5 minutes, until beans begin to wrinkle. Remove to bowl. Cover; keep warm.

- Add remaining oil to pan; heat over medium-high heat. Add chicken; stir-fry until white, about 3 minutes. Add green-bean mixture, broth, lemon juice, and salt; stir-fry until heated through. Pour into serving dish; sprinkle with peanuts.

Per Serving: 317 calories, 9g carbohydrates, 32g protein, 18g fat

PREP TIME: 10 MINUTES   COOKING TIME: 19 MINUTES

Grilled Turkey & Tomato Burgers

MAKES 4 SERVINGS

Fire up the barbecue and get ready for these vegetable-packed, tasty turkey burgers.

1 egg white

1/4 cup fine dry breadcrumbs

1/4 cup finely shredded carrot

1/4 cup finely chopped onion

1/4 cup finely chopped green pepper

1/2 teaspoon salt

1/8 teaspoon pepper

1 pound ground turkey

2 tablespoons grated Parmesan cheese

nonstick cooking spray

1 medium tomato, sliced

● In a large bowl combine the egg white, breadcrumbs and, if using beef, 2 tablespoons water. Stir in the carrot, onion, green pepper, salt, and pepper. Add the ground meat and Parmesan cheese and mix well. Shape meat mixture into four 3/4-inch-thick patties.

● Prepare an outdoor grill for barbecue. When the coals are ready, grease a cold grill rack with nonstick cooking spray and place the rack on a grill. Grill the burgers over medium coals for 7 minutes. Turn and grill 8 to 11 minutes or until no pink remains. Place 1 tomato slice on each burger and grill 1 minute longer.

Per serving: 227 calories, 9g carbohydrates, 23g protein, 11g fat

QUICK COOKS' TIP:

You can shape these burgers ahead of time and keep them refrigerated until you are ready to cook them.

PREP TIME: 10 MINUTES COOKING TIME: 15 MINUTES

Stir-Fried Turkey and Vegetables

MAKES 4 SERVINGS

Cook the vegetables until just tender and crisp. They will be juicier and more interesting with a little crunch.

12 ounces of turkey breasts

2 tablespoons sunflower oil

1 medium onion, sliced

2 garlic cloves, finely chopped

1 red bell pepper, seeded and finely sliced

1 cup mushrooms, sliced

2 tablespoons sherry

1 teaspoon cornstarch

1 (8-ounce) package baby spinach leaves

2 tablespoons soy sauce

1 teaspoon dark sesame oil

salt to taste

freshly ground pepper to taste

• Pound the turkey gently between two pieces of plastic wrap. Remove the plastic and cut the turkey into thin strips. Heat the oil in a large skillet and cook the turkey breasts for 3 minutes. Remove from the pan and keep warm.

• Add 1 tablespoon of oil to the pan and stir-fry the onion, garlic, red pepper, and mushrooms for 2 to 3 minutes.

• Blend the sherry with the cornstarch in a cup and gradually stir it into the onion mixture. Add the turkey and spinach and cook gently until the spinach wilts, 7 to 8 minutes. Stir in the soy sauce and sesame oil. Season with salt and pepper.

Per serving: 256 calories, 9g carbohydrates, 22g protein, 14g fat

Honey Turkey Fajitas

MAKES 8 SERVINGS

You can substitute chicken breast or pork tenderloin for the turkey. These margarita-inspired seasonings go well with many meats.

1 pound (uncooked) turkey breast

juice and grated rind of 1 lime

juice of 1 orange

1 red chili pepper, finely diced

2 tablespoons tequila

2 tablespoons olive oil

1 tablespoon strong-flavored honey

*1 teaspoon chopped fresh cilantro, plus additional
    for serving*

salt and pepper to taste

8 warm flour tortillas

*1 (8-ounce) container crème fraîche or sour cream
    for serving*

• Cut the turkey into strips no longer than your little finger. Place in a large bowl and add the lime juice and grated rind, orange juice, chili, tequila, oil, honey, and 1 teaspoon cilantro. Mix well. Cover and marinate in the refrigerator for 4 to 6 hours.

• When ready to serve, heat a heavy, nonstick skillet. Drain the turkey, reserving the marinade. Add the turkey to the skillet and cook rapidly to brown quickly. Add the marinade and heat to boiling over medium-high heat while stirring the turkey. Cook until the turkey is glazed and the marinade has sizzled away. Season with salt and pepper.

• Sprinkle the tortillas with a little water and heat for 30 seconds in another skillet. Place a little turkey on each tortilla, fold up and serve with a little crème fraîche and chopped cilantro.

**Per serving: 292 calories, 20g carbohydrates,
16g protein, 15g fat**

Turkey Piccata

MAKES 4 SERVINGS

Meyer lemons have a unique flavor because they are a cross between an orange and a lemon. So you get the familiar aroma and acidity without the pucker!

1 lemon (Meyer lemons preferred), zest and juice

1/4 cup all-purpose flour

salt and freshly ground pepper

1 1/2 pounds turkey cutlets

1 1/2 tablespoons butter

1 1/2 tablespoons olive oil

1/4 cup dry white wine

1 tablespoon chopped fresh Italian parsley

2 teaspoons drained small capers

lemon wedges for serving (Meyer lemon preferred)

• Grate 2 teaspoons zest from lemon; squeeze juice and strain. Set aside. Mix flour with 1/4 teaspoon each salt and pepper on waxed paper. Coat cutlets on one side with mixture; shake off excess.

• Melt butter in oil in large nonstick skillet over medium-high heat; when butter stops bubbling, fry cutlets floured side down until juice beads form on top and bottom is golden, 1 to 2 minutes. Turn cutlets over; fry until golden on underside, 1 to 2 minutes. Remove to warm plate; drizzle with lemon juice. Cover loosely with foil; keep warm.

• Add wine to hot skillet; boil over high heat until syrupy, stirring to clean pan. Stir in lemon zest, parsley and capers; pour over cutlets. Serve with lemon wedges.

Per serving: 233 calories, 3g carbohydrates, 25g protein, 13g fat

PREP TIME: 5 MINUTES   MARINATING TIME: 10 MINUTES   COOKING TIME: 7 MINUTES

Spicy Turkey Lettuce Wraps

MAKES 4 SERVINGS

With these wraps, you'll sneak some extra vegetables without losing flavor!

8 ounces ground lean turkey

1 tablespoon soy sauce

1 tablespoon dry sherry or water

1 teaspoon cornstarch

1 teaspoon dark sesame oil

2 green onions, trimmed

8 peeled fresh or canned water chestnuts,
    rinsed and quartered

1/4 cup water

1 tablespoon peanut oil or vegetable oil

1 garlic clove, crushed through a press

2 teaspoons grated peeled fresh gingerroot

1/2 teaspoon crushed red-pepper flakes

16 leaves Boston or Bibb lettuce

• Mix turkey with soy sauce, sherry, 1/2 teaspoon cornstarch, and sesame oil in medium bowl. Marinate 10 minutes.

• Quarter onions lengthwise; cut into 1-inch pieces. Place in bowl; add water chestnuts. Mix remaining cornstarch with the water. Set aside.

• To cook: Heat oil in wok or nonstick skillet over medium-high heat. Add garlic, gingerroot, and pepper flakes; stir-fry 1 minute. Add turkey and onion mixtures; stir-fry until turkey is cooked through, 2 to 3 minutes. Stir cornstarch and water again; pour around sides of turkey; stir-fry until mixture has thickened and formed a shiny glaze. Serve in lettuce leaves.

Per Serving: 252 calories, 10g carbohydrates, 25g protein, 12g fat

Fish

Marinated Squid Salad

MAKES 5 SERVINGS

This spicy salad is called laab in Thai. Instead of squid, you can use other seafood, such as medium-size peeled shrimp, or poultry, beef, or lamb. The toasted rice powder keeps the dressing from becoming watery.

3 tablespoons uncooked long-grain rice

1 pound cleaned and skinned squid

1 tablespoon grated lime rind

1/4 cup fresh lime juice

2 tablespoons sliced shallots

2 tablespoons sliced green onions

2 tablespoons Thai fish sauce (nam pla)

1 teaspoon crushed red-pepper flakes

1 tablespoon chopped fresh green chile

1 tablespoon chopped fresh mint

5 lime wedges

• Toast the rice in a skillet over medium heat until browned, about 5 minutes, stirring occasionally. Place the rice in a blender and process until it is a powder. Set aside.

• Cut the squid into 1/4-inch-thick rings and set aside. Heat 4 cups water to boiling in a large saucepan. Add the squid and cook just until the rings begin to curl around edges, about 30 seconds. Drain well while rinsing with cold water. Pat dry with paper towels.

• Combine the squid, lime rind and juice, shallots, green onions, fish sauce, and pepper flakes in a bowl and toss gently to mix. Spoon onto a serving platter and sprinkle with the chopped chile and mint. Serve with lime wedges for squeezing onto the salad.

Per serving: 115 calories, 10 g carbohydrate, 15g protein, 1g fat

PREP TIME: 15 MINUTES   COOKING TIME: 15 MINUTES

Baked Fish and Vegetable Packets

MAKES 6 SERVINGS

This recipe is fast, simple, and guaranteed to be a hit!

6 large romaine leaves

1 medium carrot, shredded

1 1/2 cups shredded coleslaw mix or a mix of
   shredded red and green cabbage and carrots

2 teaspoons balsamic vinegar

1 1/2 pounds cod or halibut filets, cut into 6 square
   pieces (they don't have to be exact, they just
   shouldn't be strips)

salt and freshly ground pepper

2 tablespoons butter

• Preheat oven to 400 degrees. Blanch romaine leaves in boiling water 1 minute; drain in colander and place in bowl of ice and water until cold. Drain; place on work surface.

• Pile 1/4 cup coleslaw mix near root end of romaine leaves. Drizzle with vinegar. Top with a piece of fish. Sprinkle with salt and pepper.

• Grease a 2-quart shallow baking dish with some of the butter; dot the remainder over the fish. Fold stem end of romaine up over the fish; fold sides over. Roll up, egg-roll fashion. Place seam side down in prepared dish. Cover with foil; bake until fish is cooked through, 25 to 30 minutes.

Per serving: 121 calories, 2g carbohydrates, 17g protein, 5g fat

Fruits of the Garden & Sea En Papillote

MAKES 4 SERVINGS

You'll enjoy serving and devouring these surprise packages. All the aromas, flavors, and juices stay sealed inside the parchment paper.

3/4 cup fresh corn kernels

1/2 cup coarsely shredded carrot

1/4 cup frozen green peas, thawed

1/4 cup sliced scallions

8 ounces cod or other lean white fish fillet, cut into
    1-inch pieces

12 large shrimp (3/4 pound), peeled and deveined

4 large sea scallops (1/2 pound)

1/4 teaspoon salt

1/8 teaspoon freshly ground pepper

2 tablespoons freshly grated Parmesan cheese

2 tablespoons fresh lemon juice

• Preheat the oven to 425 degrees. Combine the corn, carrot, peas, and scallions in a bowl and mix well.

• Cut 4 (15-inch) squares of parchment paper. Fold each square in half, open each one and place 1/4 cup of the corn mixture near the fold. Arrange one-fourth of the cod, 3 shrimp, and 1 scallop in a single layer over the corn mixture and sprinkle the salt and pepper evenly over the seafood. Spoon an additional 1/4 cup corn mixture over each serving, top each with 1 1/2 teaspoons cheese, and drizzle with the lemon juice.

• Fold the paper and seal the edges with narrow folds. Place the packets on a baking sheet.

• Bake the packets until puffed and lightly browned, about 11 minutes. Place the packets on individual serving plates, cut open, and serve immediately.

Per serving: 229 calories, 11g carbohydrates, 39g protein, 2g fat

Mussels with Spicy Cucumber Sauce

MAKES 4 SERVINGS

This traditional dish is given a very tasty update with a terrific blend of spices and the tang of cucumber.

2 *pounds mussels, scrubbed and de-bearded*

1/4 cup dry white vermouth

1 cup crème fraîche

1/4 cup finely chopped green onions

2 tablespoons grated fresh gingerroot

1/2 teaspoon curry powder

salt and ground white pepper to taste

1 European cucumber

- Combine mussels and vermouth in large deep skillet and heat to boiling. Cover and steam 2 minutes. Stir to make sure all mussels are positioned so they can open. Steam 2 minutes or until mussels open. Discard unopened mussels. Cool mussels in broth.

- Remove mussels from shells and place in a large bowl. Strain cooking broth through a sieve lined with a double thickness of cheesecloth into a small saucepan to remove any sand from mussels.

- Place crème fraiche in medium bowl; add strained broth, green onions, gingerroot, curry powder, salt, and pepper. Mix well; pour over mussels. Cut cucumber in half lengthwise; scoop out seeds with a teaspoon. Thinly slice cucumber and add to mussel mixture; toss to coat.

Per serving: 249 calories, 10g carbohydrates, 16g protein, 13g fat

PREP TIME: 5 MINUTES   COOKING TIME: 6 TO 9 MINUTES

Grilled Bluefish with Meyer Lemon

MAKES 4 SERVINGS

The most difficult part of this recipe is firing up the grill!

2 pounds bluefish fillets (2 large or 4 small), skinned
3 Meyer lemons, two halved, one quartered
1/4 cup mayonnaise
salt
2 tablespoons crushed pink peppercorns
1/4 cup fresh cilantro leaves for serving

• Preheat broiler or prepare outdoor grill for barbecue. Place fillets skinned side down in foil-lined roasting pan or in oiled fish grill. (Place fish grill on baking sheet.)

• Squeeze the juice from half the citrus halves over the fish. Slather with mayonnaise and sprinkle with salt and peppercorns. Close grill and clamp handle if using fish grill. Broil or grill so that top of fish is 4 inches from heat source until cooked through, 6 to 9 minutes, according to thickness of fish. (If top of fish starts to brown too much before fish is cooked, move rack down a level.)

• Sprinkle fish with cilantro. Serve with lemon quarters.

Per serving: 333 calories, 5g carbohydrates, 44g protein, 14g fat

PREP TIME: 10 MINUTES   COOKING TIME: 5 MINUTES

Sherry-Steamed Fish

MAKES 4 SERVINGS

The fish nicely absorbs the sherry, which makes for a savory flavor.

4 (6-ounce) skinless mild fish fillets (flounder, fluke, or rainbow trout)
1/2 teaspoon fine sea salt
2 tablespoons sweet sherry
2 teaspoons low-sodium soy sauce plus extra for serving
2 green onions, trimmed, finely chopped
2 tablespoons sliced pickled ginger or slivered fresh peeled gingerroot

• Gently rinse fish in a bowl of water; pat dry. Fold thinner ends under fillets and place in a shallow bowl that will fit into a wok or steamer. Sprinkle fish with salt. Mix sherry and soy sauce; pour over fish. Sprinkle with onions and ginger.

• Place bowl in wok or steamer rack over boiling water. Cover and steam until cooked through, about 5 minutes. Carefully remove lid and serve immediately.

Per serving: 116 calories, 2g carbohydrates, 21g protein, 1g fat

Alaskan Salmon Salad Sandwiches

MAKES 6 SERVINGS

These are lunchtime fare but fancy enough for little tea sandwiches. The tangy yogurt and lemon juice in the dressing brightens the mixture more than mayonnaise could.

1 (15¹/2-ounce) can Alaskan salmon
1/3 cup plain nonfat yogurt
1/3 cup chopped scallions
1/3 cup chopped celery
1 tablespoon lemon juice
freshly ground pepper to taste
6 pita loaves

● Drain the salmon and place in a large bowl. Separate into flakes using a fork. Stir in the yogurt, scallions, celery, lemon juice, and pepper and mix well.

● Cut a slice off of a pita edge so you can open it. Place the slice at the bottom of the pocket to help absorb the juices from the filling. Repeat with the remaining pitas.

● To serve, spoon the salad into the pitas.

Per serving: 189 calories, 17g carbohydrates, 18g protein, 5g fat

Broiled Scallops with Wasabi and Ginger Butter

MAKES 4 SERVINGS

The classic Japanese flavor combination of ginger and horseradish pairs nicely with scallops.

WASABI AND GINGER BUTTER:

2 tablespoons powdered wasabi (Japanese
*   horseradish), prepared wasabi, or freshly grated*
*   peeled wasabi*

2 tablespoons pickled ginger, slivered, with juices

1 tablespoon fresh lime juice

4 tablespoons butter, whisked until creamy for
*   easier blending*

16 large sea scallops (2 pounds)

2 tablespoons soy sauce

• Make Wasabi and Ginger Butter: Blend wasabi with ginger and juices. Stir in butter until blended. Use immediately or pack into a ramekin or roll up in butter wrapper into a 1-inch cylinder. Chill or freeze until firm.

• Place scallops on rack in broiler pan. Brush on both sides with soy sauce. Broil 4 inches from heat source until browned, about 3 minutes on each side.

• Slice wasabi butter into 16 rounds; place one on each scallop.

Per serving: 312 calories, 8g carbohydrates, 39g protein, 13g fat

Oysters over Grilled Fennel

MAKES 6 SERVINGS

These oysters are as tasty as they are easy to prepare!

1 bulb fennel, trimmed, cut lengthwise into 6 slices

olive oil for brushing

salt and freshly ground pepper

cayenne pepper for dusting

1 pint shucked oysters, undrained

4 ounces thick bacon, cut into 1/4-inch lardons

1/4 cup finely chopped red onion

1/4 cup finely chopped green bell pepper

1/4 cup finely chopped celery

1 tablespoon flour

1/2 cup heavy cream

1 tablespoon anise-flavored liqueur, such as Pernod,
    or more to taste

grated zest and 1 tablespoon juice of 1 lemon,
    preferably a Meyer lemon, and wedges for serving

Tabasco sauce to taste

1 tablespoon finely chopped parsley

• Preheat broiler. Place fennel slices on baking sheet; brush on both sides with oil and sprinkle with salt, pepper, and cayenne. Broil until browned and tender, about 3 minutes on each side. Keep warm.

• Poach oysters in their liquor over medium heat in a saucepan until their edges curl, about 3 minutes. Remove from heat.

• In large skillet, sauté bacon over medium-high heat until crisp; remove to paper towels; keep warm. In drippings, sauté onion, bell pepper, and celery until tender, about 3 minutes; stir in flour and cook until fragrant, 1 minute. Stir in 1/2 cup oyster liquor; cook until boiling. Stir in cream, anise liqueur, lemon juice, Tabasco, and pepper; heat to boiling. Stir in oysters; heat through (do not overcook).

• To serve: Spoon oysters and sauce over grilled fennel. Sprinkle with bacon and parsley.

Per serving: 192 calories, 10g carbohydrates, 6g protein, 14g fat

PREP TIME: 15 MINUTES   COOKING TIME: 5 MINUTES

Grilled Trout with Horseradish Crust

MAKES 2 SERVINGS

Enjoy the crunch of a crust without the carbs!

2 skinless trout fillets

1 tablespoon olive oil plus extra for greasing the pan

1 slice whole-wheat bread, ground into small,
   coarse crumbs

2 teaspoons creamed horseradish

1 tablespoon chopped fresh parsley

grated rind of 1/2 lemon

FOR THE DRESSING

1 teaspoon Dijon mustard

juice of 1/2 lemon

salt to taste

freshly ground pepper to taste

2 tablespoons virgin olive oil

1 cup mixed crisp salad leaves

• Preheat the broiler. Brush a broiler pan with oil. Sprinkle the trout fillets with salt and pepper.

• In a bowl, mix together the bread, horseradish, parsley, 1 tablespoon olive oil, and the lemon rind. Spread this mixture over the trout fillets and place under the grill for 5 minutes to cook.

• For the dressing: Mix the mustard and lemon juice together in a bowl. Add a little salt and pepper and whisk in the oil very slowly. Mix the salad leaves with a little of the dressing and place on a large dinner plate. Drizzle the remaining dressing around the outside of the plate. Place the crusted trout on top of the salad leaves and serve warm.

Per serving: 358 calories, 10g carbohydrates, 21g protein, 29g fat

Halibut with Balsamic Tarragon Glaze

MAKES 4 SERVINGS

Quick. Tasty. Why not make it, just for the "halibut?"

1/4 cup olive oil

4 (8-ounce) halibut fillets

fine sea salt

freshly ground black pepper

1 tablespoon fresh torn tarragon leaves

1/4 cup balsamic vinegar

• Heat oil in large skillet over medium-high heat. Sprinkle fish on both sides with salt and pepper. Fry on both sides until cooked through, about 8 minutes in all. Remove fish to warm platter; cover.

• Add tarragon and vinegar to hot skillet; boil over high heat until thickened slightly, about 3 minutes. Pour over fish.

Per serving: 505 calories, 1g carbohydrates, 29g protein, 42g fat

Broiled Gingered Tuna

MAKES 4 SERVINGS

No time to marinate? That's ok, because this simple glaze is so packed full of flavor that there's no need to marinate the fish.

GLAZE

3 green onions, finely chopped

3 tablespoons roasted garlic teriyaki sauce

3 tablespoons mirin (sweet rice wine) or cream sherry

2 tablespoons chopped peeled fresh gingerroot, crushed through a garlic press

1 tablespoon honey

pinch of cayenne pepper

nonstick cooking spray

4 (6-ounce) boneless tuna steaks (1-inch thick)

• Prepare an outdoor grill for barbecue or preheat broiler. Mix glaze ingredients in a bowl. Grease grill rack or broiling rack with cooking spray. Place steaks on grill rack or in broiler pan; brush on both sides with glaze. Grill or broil tuna 6 inches from medium-hot coals or heat source until medium-rare (4 minutes on each side) or until desired degree of doneness, basting with remaining glaze.

Per serving: 235 calories, 6g carbohydrates, 44g protein, 1g fat

Grilled Curried Shrimp with Hot Chile Tartar Sauce

MAKES 4 SERVINGS

With this spicy ensemble, you'll be too busy quenching your thirst to miss the carbs!

2 pounds large or extra-large shrimp, shells left on, tails intact

3/4 cup plain yogurt

1 tablespoon curry powder

HOT CHILE TARTAR SAUCE:

1/4 cup mayonnaise

1 tablespoon fresh lemon juice

1 teaspoon India relish or other sweet pickle relish

1/2 teaspoon sambal oelek or more to taste

● Prepare outdoor grill for barbecue or preheat broiler. For best results, cut shrimp shells on outer curve with scissors; remove veins. Mix yogurt with curry powder in shallow bowl; add shrimp and toss to coat, pressing marinade into flesh around shells. Marinate for 15 minutes.

● Make Hot Chile Tartar Sauce: Mix mayonnaise with lemon juice, relish, and 1 teaspoon sambal oelek in a small bowl until blended. Taste and add more sambal oelek if desired.

● Grill shrimp over medium coals or heat, or broil 6 inches from heat until pink, turning once with tongs, 3 to 4 minutes in all. Serve with Hot Chile Tartar Sauce for dipping.

Per serving: 328 calories, 10g carbohydrates, 48g protein, 9g fat

Parsley and Chive-Packed Salmon Cod Cakes

MAKES 8 SERVINGS

You say potato and I say fish cake—it's an association thing. This mix of fresh herbs, fish, and yes, potatoes, makes even meat lovers agree that there are burgers, and then there are fish cakes. Let's call the whole thing delicious.

12 ounces potatoes, peeled and freshly boiled
1 ounce butter, melted
salt to taste
freshly ground pepper to taste
6 ounces salmon fillet, skinned
6 ounces cod fillet, skinned
6 scallions, peeled and finely sliced
4 tablespoons chopped fresh parsley
2 tablespoons chopped fresh chives
grated rind and juice of 1 lemon

For Frying
1 beaten egg
6 tablespoons fine fresh white breadcrumbs
1 ounce unsalted butter
4 tablespoons sunflower oil

• Mash the potatoes with the melted butter, salt, and freshly ground pepper in a medium bowl. Set aside.

• Season the salmon and cod with salt and pepper. Heat a little water and a splash of lemon juice in a shallow pan and lightly poach the seasoned salmon and cod until just cooked. Remove the fish from the cooking liquid and flake apart.

• Place the mashed potato and flaked fish into a large mixing bowl. Add the scallions, herbs, lemon rind and chives and mix well. Taste and adjust the seasoning if necessary. Roll teaspoonfuls of the mixture into balls and flatten the top and sides with a small spatula to form small fish cakes. Pour the beaten egg onto a plate and the breadcrumbs onto a second plate. Dip the fish cakes first in the beaten egg and then in the bread-crumbs to coat. Pat smooth with a small spatula.

• Heat a cast-iron or heavy base skillet. Melt the butter in the oil over medium heat and fry the fish cakes on all sides until crisp, golden, and hot, about 4 minutes for each side. Cook in two batches, keeping the first batch hot while cooking the second. Drain on paper towels. Serve with lemon wedges or perhaps a parsley sauce.

Per serving: 224 calories, 11g carbohydrates, 11g protein, 15g fat

QUICK COOKS' TIP:

The directions call for using a metal spatula to shape the fish cakes. This is really the key to shaping them, because using your hands actually warms the fish mixture and makes it sticky and more difficult to shape. Use two spatulas for speed and efficiency. Soon you will become the neighborhood fish-cake meister, and, you've been warned, there's no turning back!

PREP TIME: 5 MINUTES   COOKING TIME: 15 MINUTES

Pan-Fried Snapper with Sake Teriyaki Sauce

MAKES 4 SERVINGS

The sweetness of the wine and the saltiness of the soy sauce make for a striking balance in this scrumptious dish.

2 tablespoons olive oil
4 thick red snapper fillets (8 ounces each) with
   skin on
fine sea salt
freshly ground pepper

SAKE TERIYAKI SAUCE
1 cup sake
1/4 cup mirin (sweet rice wine) or dry sherry
1/4 cup soy sauce
1 tablespoon sugar

• Preheat oven to 400 degrees. Heat oil in ovenproof skillet over medium-high heat. Sprinkle snapper with salt and pepper on both sides; place skin side down in skillet. Press fillets with 2 long metal spatulas or pancake turners and hold down gently 1 minute so skin stays flat in pan. Cook 3 minutes, until skin is crisp; turn over. Cook 1 minute. Place in oven to finish cooking, about 3 minutes.

• While fish cooks, make Sake Teriyaki Sauce: Combine ingredients in 2-quart saucepan; heat to simmering over medium heat. Simmer until reduced to 1/2 cup.

• To serve: Place snapper skin side up on plates; pour sauce around each.

Per serving: 346 calories, 4g carbohydrates, 47g protein, 10g fat

Stir-Fried Lemongrass Shrimp

MAKES 4 SERVINGS

The lemony tang nicely complements the shrimp.

LEMONGRASS DIPPING SAUCE

2/3 cup vegetable broth, fish stock, or water

2 tablespoons minced lemongrass (tender insides only)

1 tablespoon minced chives

1 tablespoon light soy sauce

1 teaspoon cornstarch

salt to taste

2 tablespoons vegetable oil

1 1/2 pounds raw unpeeled jumbo shrimp (tails intact)

1 bunch thin green onions, trimmed, cut into
   1-inch pieces

1 medium red bell pepper, seeded, thinly sliced

2 tablespoons dry sherry

2 tablespoons water

● Make Lemongrass Dipping Sauce: Combine ingredients in small saucepan until blended. Heat to boiling, stirring until clear and thickened. Taste and add more salt if needed. Keep warm.

● Heat wok or large heavy skillet over medium-high heat. Add oil and when almost smoking, add shrimp, onions, and pepper. Stir-fry 2 minutes using long chopsticks or Chinese stir-fry shovel. Add sherry and water. Stir-fry until shrimp are pink and curled, 1 to 2 minutes. Serve with sauce for dipping.

Per serving: 275 calories, 6g carbohydrates, 36g protein, 10g fat

Pasta

Linguine with Tuna, Lemon & Arugula •

Asian Sesame Noodles with Vegetables •

Toasted Quinoa with Cheese •

Fresh Salmon Lasagne with Tomato Dressing •

Couscous with Asparagus •

• Spiced Kasha and Radicchio

• Spaghetti Squash Carbonara

• Cellophane Noodles with
  Garlic-Peanut Sauce

• Egg Noodles with Chicken & Vegetables

Linguine with Tuna, Lemon & Arugula

4 FIRST-COURSE SERVINGS

Combining pasta and fish is always a winner. Arugula adds an extra zip to an already delicious dish!

3 tablespoons extra-virgin olive oil

2 garlic cloves, finely chopped

1 small dried red chile, crushed

1 (7-ounce) can tuna in olive oil, drained and flaked

4 ounces linguine

1 bunch arugula, washed and dried, leaves coarsely chopped

juice of 1 lemon, or to taste

salt to taste

• In a 3-quart saucepan, heat the oil over medium-low heat and gently cook the garlic and chile. As the garlic begins to change color, add the tuna and stir. Keep warm.

• Cook the pasta in 2 quarts of boiling salted water in a deep skillet. When the pasta is al dente, add the arugula and immediately drain the pasta and arugula in a colander. Add the pasta mixture to the tuna mixture. Drizzle with half the lemon juice. Using two wooden spoons, lift up and stir pasta and arugula until the tuna is evenly distributed. Taste and add more lemon juice and salt if needed. Serve at once.

Per serving: 257 calories, 20g carbohydrates, 18g protein, 12g fat

Asian Sesame Noodles with Vegetables

MAKES 8 SERVINGS

Always a favorite, sesame noodles and vegetables make a classic, winning combination.

SAUCE:

2 green onions, trimmed, cut into 2-inch pieces

2 cloves garlic, peeled

1/4 cup sesame tahini

1/4 cup vegetable broth or chicken broth

1/4 cup fresh lemon juice

1/4 cup low-sodium soy sauce

1/2 teaspoon crushed red pepper flakes, or more
   to taste

1 (16-ounce) bag coleslaw mix (shredded red and
   green cabbage and carrots)

1 cup slender green beans, trimmed

4 ounces Hong Kong–style fresh egg noodles or
   fresh angel hair pasta

2 tablespoons Asian (dark) sesame oil

chopped roasted peanuts

• Heat 2 quarts of salted water to boiling in large deep skillet or wide pot.

• While water heats, start sauce: Finely chop green onions and garlic in food processor. Add remaining ingredients; purée.

• Add cole slaw mix and beans to boiling water; cook 1 minute. Add pasta; cook 3 minutes. Drain, reserving 3/4 cup cooking water. Place slaw mix in bowl; toss with sesame oil.

• Blend enough vegetable cooking water into the sauce to make a thin coating. Taste and toss with more salt if needed. Pour over vegetable-noodle mixture; toss to coat.

Per serving: 142 calories, 16g carbohydrates, 5g protein, 8g fat

PREP TIME: 10 MINUTES   COOKING TIME: 30 MINUTES

Toasted Quinoa with Cheese

MAKES 6 SERVINGS

A South American staple, particularly in Peru, quinoa is a pigweed found in the high Andes.

1/3 cup quinoa

2 cups hot vegetable or chicken broth (from bouillon cubes is fine)

3 tablespoons fruity olive oil

2 tablespoons red-wine vinegar

1/2 teaspoon crushed red-pepper flakes

salt and freshly ground black pepper to taste

1 cup chopped celery

1 cup shredded Monterey Jack with jalapeños

1/4 cup chopped carrots

1/4 cup chopped green onions

2 tablespoons sliced black olives

● Preheat oven to 325 degrees. Place quinoa in fine sieve; rinse well. Spread out on a baking sheet; bake 15 minutes, until fragrant and toasty, stirring once or twice.

● Place quinoa in 2-quart saucepan. Add broth; heat to boiling over medium-high heat. Reduce heat to medium-low and simmer until quinoa is tender, about 15 minutes. Scrape into a large bowl.

● While quinoa cooks, whisk together oil, vinegar, and pepper flakes until blended. Season with salt and pepper. Pour over quinoa; toss to coat using a rubber spatula. Add celery, cheese, carrots, and olives; mix well. Taste, and adjust salt and pepper if needed.

Per serving: 191 calories, 9g carbohydrates, 8g protein, 14g fat

Fresh Salmon Lasagne with Tomato Dressing

MAKES 4 SERVINGS

This is an easy-to-make, glamorous to serve entrée. If beefsteak tomatoes are out of season, use eight of the ripest plum tomatoes you can find.

DRESSING

3 beefsteak tomatoes, chopped

1/2 cup olive oil

1/3 cup balsamic vinegar

1/4 cup snipped fresh chives plus 8 whole chives
    for garnish

salt to taste

freshly ground pepper to taste

nonstick cooking spray

8 (3-ounce) thin slices fresh salmon fillets

8 cooked short lasagne noodles, warm

● For the dressing, combine the tomatoes, oil, vinegar, and snipped chives in a small saucepan. Season with salt and pepper and heat through. Keep warm.

● Grease a nonstick skillet with cooking spray. Pan-fry the salmon until just heated through, about 1 minute on each side. On each of 4 dinner plates, place a piece of salmon, then top with a noodle, then a piece of salmon, and then another noodle. Spoon some warm dressing over each portion and criss cross 2 whole chives over each.

Per serving: 623 calories, 20g carbohydrates, 40g protein, 42g fat

PREP TIME: 10 MINUTES   COOKING TIME: 1 MINUTE
STANDING TIME: 5 MINUTES

Couscous with Asparagus

MAKES 8 SERVINGS

Couscous is a quick-cooking grain that always adds an exotic flair to any meal.

8 ounces fresh asparagus, trimmed, cut into
   1-inch pieces
1/2 teaspoon salt or to taste
3/4 cup couscous
8 ounces cauliflower florets, shredded in food
   processor or with grater
4 ounces sliced mushrooms (any kind)
4 tablespoons butter, in small pieces
2 tablespoons chopped flat-leaf parsley
1 tablespoon grated lemon zest

• Bring 1 3/4 cups water to boiling in small saucepan; add the salt and asparagus and boil 1 minute. Remove asparagus with slotted spoon to a bowl of ice water.

• Add couscous, cauliflower, mushrooms, and butter to water. Stir, cover, and remove from heat. Drain asparagus and add to couscous. Fluff with fork. Let stand at least 5 minutes.

• To serve: Taste couscous and adjust salt if needed. Spoon into serving dish; sprinkle with parsley and lemon zest.

Per serving: 129 calories, 16g carbohydrates, 4g protein, 6g fat

PREP TIME: 10 MINUTES   COOKING TIME: 15 MINUTES

Spiced Kasha and Radicchio

MAKES 8 SERVINGS

Radicchio instantly dresses up this simple kasha porridge.

3 tablespoons olive oil
1/4 cup chopped red onion
1/2 cup whole kasha
1 teaspoon ground cinnamon
1 teaspoon caraway seeds, crushed
1 1/2 cups water or vegetable broth
2 cups shredded radicchio
1/4 cup chopped dried apples
1 tablespoon red-wine vinegar or more to taste
freshly ground pepper to taste
salt to taste if needed

• Heat oil in a large skillet over medium-high heat. Add onion, kasha, cinnamon, and caraway; sauté until onions start to soften, about 3 minutes. Add water; heat to boiling. Simmer, mostly covered, over medium heat, until kasha is softened, about 10 minutes.

• Stir radicchio, apples, vinegar, and pepper into kasha; cover. Cook until radicchio is wilted and apples plump. Taste and adjust seasoning if needed.

Per serving: 93 calories, 10g carbohydrates, 1.5g protein, 6g fat

PREP TIME: 5 MINUTES   MICROWAVING TIME: 12 MINUTES   STANDING TIME: 5 MINUTES   COOKING TIME: 10 MINUTES

Spaghetti Squash Carbonara

MAKES 8 SERVINGS

Spaghetti squash is always a delightful substitute for pasta.

1/2 of a 3-pound spaghetti squash, seeds scooped out
1/4 cup water
2 tablespoons butter
6 ounces smoked ham, diced
3 eggs
1 cup heavy cream
2/3 cup freshly grated Parmigiano-Reggiano cheese
salt and freshly ground pepper to taste
2 tablespoons chopped fresh Italian flat-leaf parsley

• Place squash cut side up in glass baking dish; add 1/4 cup water to dish. Pierce squash on all sides with fork or metal skewer. Cover with plastic wrap; vent. Cook on high 12 minutes, turning dish every 4 minutes, until squash is tender. Let stand 5 minutes. Scoop out "spaghetti" with fork. Place in large warm bowl; cover and keep warm.

• While squash cooks, melt butter in large nonstick skillet. Add ham; sauté until lightly browned, about 5 minutes.

• In a medium bowl, beat eggs with cream until blended but not frothy. Pour egg mixture into skillet; heat over low heat, stirring constantly with a wooden spoon; do not scramble eggs; just keep them moving until firm, about 5 minutes.

• Stir cheese into egg mixture. Season with salt and pepper. Add to squash; toss with wooden salad forks to mix. Sprinkle with parsley.

Per serving: 196 calories, 8g carbohydrates, 11g protein, 14g fat

Cellophane Noodles with Garlic-Peanut Sauce

MAKES 8 SERVINGS

These noodles are also called bean thread noodles because they are made from mung beans. They are found in Chinese grocery stores and are packaged in bundles of varying weights.

2 (2-ounce) bundles Chinese rice vermicelli noodles

1 cup creamy peanut butter

1 cup chicken or vegetable broth, or more if necessary

3 tablespoons rice vinegar

2 tablespoons dark sesame oil

2 tablespoons minced fresh cilantro

2 tablespoons soy sauce

1 teaspoon minced garlic

1/2 teaspoon sugar

1/2 teaspoon dry mustard

4 scallions (white and green parts), cut into
   1/2-inch pieces

2 tablespoons toasted sesame seeds

● Cut the noodles with scissors into 5-inch or 6-inch lengths. Place them in a metal or other heatproof bowl and cover with boiling water. Allow them to soften, stirring occasionally, for 5 minutes. Drain in a colander and refresh under cold running water. Dry by patting with paper towels and place in a shallow serving bowl.

● Combine the peanut butter and 1/2 cup of the broth, the vinegar, oil, cilantro, soy sauce, garlic, sugar, and mustard in a blender. Blend until smooth, starting out using a pulse motion. With the machine running, pour in 1/2 cup more broth through the opening in the lid. Process until blended and smooth, adding a little more broth if necessary to give the sauce a pourable consistency.

● Pour the peanut sauce over the noodles and toss to coat well. Sprinkle with scallions and the sesame seeds and toss again. Serve at room temperature.

Per serving: 295 calories, 20g carbohydrates, 9g protein, 21g fat

Egg Noodles with Chicken & Vegetables

MAKES 8 FIRST-COURSE SERVINGS

6 ounces dried Chinese egg noodles

8 ounces chicken breast

1 medium carrot, peeled and julienned

4 ounces green beans, trimmed and cut in half
    lengthwise

1 cup julienned daikon radish

2 tablespoons soy sauce

1 tablespoon oyster sauce

1 tablespoon oil

1 red chile, sliced (optional)

2 sprigs fresh cilantro, leaves only

● Soak the noodles in boiling water until softened, about 1 minute. Drain in a colander and rinse well with cold water. Squeeze off excess water. Slice the chicken breast into thin pieces.

● Heat the oil in a wok over medium-high heat and add the chicken pieces and vegetables. Stir-fry until the chicken is almost cooked through. Add the noodles and heat through. Add the soy sauce and the oyster sauce and stir-fry until the chicken and noodles are coated. Let cook 2 minutes, until heated through and the chicken is cooked.

● Turn out the noodle mixture onto a serving plate and garnish with the slices of chile and cilantro leaves. Serve hot.

Per serving: 145 calories, 18g carbohydrates, 11g protein, 3g fat

Vegetables & Side Dishes

Roasted Chioggia Beets with Feta & Raspberry Vinegar

Grilled Radicchio with Gorgonzola-Walnut Sauce

Spaghetti Squash Primavera

Smoky Green Beans

Caribbean Stewed Vegetables

Grilled Portobello Mushrooms with Tomato Sauce

Eggplant with Olive Sauce

Stir-Fried Bok Choy and Mushrooms

Sautéed Cabbage with Juniper Berries

Spiced Shredded Cabbage

- Fried Okra
- Potato & Sugar Snap Pea Sauté
- Celeriac Sauté
- Roasted Asparagus with Orange Sauce
- Broccoli with Lemon-Garlic Ricotta Crumbs
- Zucchini-Pita Sandwiches with Golden Shallot-Garlic Sauce
- Sautéed Mushrooms with Pancetta
- Garlic Cauliflower Purée
- Sautéed Cucumbers
- Braised Radishes
- Mixed Vegetable Pancakes
- Sweet & Sour Carrot-Parsnip Julienne

Roasted Chioggia Beets with Feta & Raspberry Vinegar

MAKES 8 SERVINGS

Chioggia beets give tangy feta cheese a sweet accent. Use imported sheep's milk cheese to get the best flavor.

1/2 cup raspberry vinegar

3 tablespoons honey

1 medium shallot, minced

kosher salt

coarsely cracked black pepper

1/4 cup grapeseed oil

8 small beets, washed and trimmed

1 tablespoon unsalted butter, cut into small bits

4 ounces feta cheese, thinly sliced

1 handful spicy baby greens, such as mizuna,
*   for garnish*

• Preheat the oven to 350 degrees. In a medium bowl, whisk together 1/4 cup of the raspberry vinegar, 11/2 tablespoons of the honey, the shallot, 1/2 teaspoon of salt and 1/2 teaspoon of pepper. Whisk in the grapeseed oil until emulsified.

• Arrange the beets so they fit snugly in a single layer in a deep baking dish. Add enough water to barely cover the beets and add the remaining 1/4 cup of vinegar and 11/2 tablespoons of honey and the butter. Season with salt and pepper. Cover with foil and bake for 50 to 60 minutes, or until the beets are tender when pierced with a knife. Let cool slightly.

• Drain and peel the beets and slice them 1/4 inch thick. Add them to the honey dressing and let marinate for up to 4 hours.

• To serve, arrange half the beet slices on 8 small plates and cover with the feta. Top with the remaining beet slices and drizzle each serving with about 1 tablespoon of the dressing. Garnish with the greens and serve.

Per serving: 172 calories, 16g carbohydrates, 4g protein, 11g fat

Grilled Radicchio with Gorgonzola-Walnut Sauce

MAKES 4 SERVINGS

While great in mixed greens, radicchio on its own can also be scrumptious.

2 medium heads radicchio (1 pound total)
salt
oil for basting

GORGONZOLA-WALNUT SAUCE:
4 ounces Gorgonzola cheese, crumbled
4 tablespoons unsalted butter, cut into pieces
1 cup light cream or half-and-half
1/4 teaspoon cracked pepper
1/2 cup chopped walnuts

● Preheat outdoor grill for barbecue or preheat broiler. Heat 3 cups salted water to boiling in medium saucepan. Cut radicchio heads in half through the cores. Blanch in the boiling water 1 minute, until wilted. Drain in colander. Place on grill or broiler pan; brush with oil. Grill 6 inches from heat source 10 minutes, turning every few minutes, until lightly browned. (If radicchio browns too quickly, move to cooler part of grill or on a lower rack.)

● Make Gorgonzola-Walnut Sauce: Combine cheese, butter, cream, and pepper in small saucepan over medium heat until smooth, whisking occasionally. Stir in nuts just before using. Serve over radicchio.

Per serving: 380 calories, 5g carbohydrates, 9g protein, 37g fat

PREP TIME: 10 MINUTES   COOKING TIME: 1 MINUTE

Spaghetti Squash Primavera

MAKES 5 SERVINGS

This vegetable alternative to pasta is deliciously juicy, crunchy, and beautifully golden. Serve chilled or at room temperature.

2 cups broccoli florets
2 cups cooked spaghetti squash
1 cup sliced fresh mushrooms
1 cup julienned yellow squash
1/4 cup sliced scallions
2 tablespoons balsamic vinegar
2 teaspoons olive oil
2 garlic cloves, crushed
1 tablespoon chopped fresh parsley
3/4 teaspoon dried basil
1/8 teaspoon salt
1/8 teaspoon freshly ground pepper
1/4 cup freshly grated fresh Parmesan cheese

● Cook the broccoli in a saucepan of boiling water for 1 minute. Drain, place in a large bowl, and add the spaghetti squash, mushrooms, and yellow squash. Toss gently and set aside.

● Whisk together the vinegar and oil in a small bowl until blended. Whisk in the garlic, parsley, basil, salt, and pepper until blended, add to the vegetable mixture, and toss well. Sprinkle with the Parmesan cheese.

Per serving: 92 calories, 11g carbohydrates, 5g protein, 4g fat

PREP TIME: 5 MINUTES   COOKING TIME: 6 MINUTES
MICROWAVING TIME: 8 MINUTES

Smoky Green Beans

MAKES 4 SERVINGS

The applewood-smoked bacon with these green beans will create a sweet and salty taste sensation!

1/4 cup diced applewood-smoked bacon
1 small onion
2 garlic cloves, crushed through a press
1 pound green beans, trimmed and halved
salt and freshly ground pepper to taste

● Cook bacon, onion, and garlic in large skillet over medium-high heat until bacon is crisp, about 6 minutes.

● While bacon cooks, combine green beans with *1/2* cup water in microwave-safe bowl or medium saucepan. Cover with plastic wrap and vent; microwave on high power until tender, about 8 minutes.

● Drain green beans, reserving cooking liquid, and add to bacon. Mix well, adding a little green bean liquid to make a juicy coating.

Per serving: 138 calories, 10g carbohydrates, 4g protein, 10g fat

Caribbean Stewed Vegetables

MAKES 12 SERVINGS

The colors and flavors of this hearty dish are as lively as the islands themselves. It tastes even better if cooked a day ahead of serving. Try it with jerked chicken and cooked rice or fresh crusty bread.

2 tablespoons vegetable oil

2 cups chopped onions

3 cups chopped cabbage

1/4 teaspoon cayenne pepper or 1 fresh chile, minced
   and seeded for a milder flavor

1 tablespoon grated peeled fresh gingerroot

3 cups peeled sweet potatoes, chopped into
   1/2-inch cubes

salt to taste

2 cups undrained chopped tomatoes, fresh or canned

2 cups sliced okra, fresh or frozen

3 tablespoons fresh lime juice

2 tablespoons chopped fresh cilantro plus (optional)
   sprigs for garnish

1 cup chopped peanuts

● Heat the oil in a dutch oven over medium heat and add the onions. Sauté until softened, 4 or 5 minutes. Add the cabbage and the cayenne or chile and sauté, stirring often, until the onions are translucent, about 8 minutes.

● Add the ginger and 2 cups water, cover, and heat to boiling. Stir in the sweet potatoes, sprinkle with salt, and simmer until the potatoes are barely tender, 5 or 6 minutes. Add the tomatoes, okra, and lime juice. Simmer until the vegetables are tender, about 15 minutes. Stir in the chopped cilantro and salt to taste.

● To serve: Sprinkle the stew with chopped peanuts. Top with a few sprigs of cilantro, if you like. Serve the stew on rice or with fresh crusty bread.

Per serving: 157 calories, 18g carbohydrates, 5g protein, 8g fat

Grilled Portobello Mushrooms with Tomato Sauce

MAKES 4 SERVINGS

Tomato sauce is a simple, fast way to go the extra mile and turn grilled mushrooms into an extremely gourmet dish!

TOMATO SAUCE

1 cup canned diced tomatoes with roasted garlic
1/2 cup chicken broth (from bouillon cube is ok)
1 tablespoon white-wine vinegar
pinch of crushed red-pepper flakes
salt and freshly ground black pepper to taste

MUSHROOMS

12 ounces sliced portobello mushroom caps
oil for drizzling (herb-, lemon- or garlic-flavored
   oil is nice)
salt and freshly ground black pepper to taste

FOR SERVING:

1/4 cup freshly grated Parmigiano-Reggiano cheese
best quality extra-virgin olive oil for drizzling

● Combine sauce ingredients in small skillet. Cover; simmer over medium-low heat 5 minutes.

● Preheat broiler. Line broiler pan with foil; spread mushrooms on top. Drizzle with oil; sprinkle with salt and pepper. Toss to coat; spread out evenly. Broil 4 inches from heat until sizzling and tender, about 10 minutes, stirring frequently.

● To serve: Spoon sauce into 4 shallow bowls. Top with mushrooms. Sprinkle with cheese; drizzle with olive oil.

Per serving: 142 calories, 8g carbohydrates, 6g protein, 10g fat

PREP TIME (INCLUDES SOAKING): 15 MINUTES   COOKING TIME: 30 MINUTES

Eggplant with Olive Sauce

MAKES 6 SERVINGS

The wide array of flavors and spices in this recipe makes for a very delectable dish!

3 to 4 celery stalks, including leaves, chopped

1 large onion, chopped

1 tablespoon salted capers

3 tablespoons olive oil

1 large (2¼-pound) eggplant, cut into 1-inch chunks

20 green olives

3 tablespoons tomato paste

1 tablespoon sugar

1 tablespoon white-wine vinegar

salt to taste

freshly ground pepper to taste

● Blanch the celery and onion in lightly salted boiling water for a few minutes and drain. Set aside.

● Meanwhile, soak the capers in a small bowl of water for 10 minutes and drain. Set aside.

● Heat half the oil in a large nonstick skillet over medium heat, add half the eggplant chunks, and fry until brown and tender. Remove to a bowl and repeat with the remaining eggplant, adding the first batch to the second when it is finished. Add the onion, celery, and all the remaining ingredients.

● Stir well, cover, and cook for about 15 minutes, adding 1 to 2 tablespoons of water if the sauce gets too thick during cooking. Remove the lid towards the end of cooking to evaporate some of the liquid if necessary. Season to taste with salt and pepper.

Per serving: 108 calories, 15g carbohydrates, 3g protein, 4g fat

PREP TIME: 15 MINUTES   COOKING TIME: 5 MINUTES

Stir-Fried Bok Choy and Mushrooms

MAKES 6 SERVINGS

The small heads of this juicy cabbage resemble a bunch of wide celery with dark green leaves. It can be used raw in salads, as a recipe ingredient, or it can be the star, as in this recipe.

1¹/2 pounds of small heads of bok choy
1 tablespoon oil
2 tablespoons oyster sauce
a dash of salt, or more to taste

• Remove the outer leaves of each bok choy head and cut crosswise into 3-inch sections (hearts) from the root end up. Wash well and drain. Separate the leaves from the stalks.

• Heat the oil in a wok over medium heat and add the stalks and a dash of salt. Stir-fry until they are softened but still crisp, about 3 minutes. Add the leaves and stir-fry until wilted.

• Add the oyster sauce and salt to taste. Stir well and serve hot.

Per serving: 39 calories, 4g carbohydrates, 1g protein, 3g fat

PREP TIME: 5 MINUTES   COOKING TIME: 5 MINUTES

Sautéed Cabbage with Juniper Berries

MAKES 6 SERVINGS

The texture of the cooked vegetables should still be really crisp and the color, bright. The cabbage can be served either hot or cold, with any meat or fish main course.

3 tablespoons chicken broth
12 juniper berries, crushed
1 green chile, seeded and chopped
1 pound green cabbage, shredded
1 green bell pepper, seeded and shredded
1 red bell pepper, seeded and shredded
2 tablespoons soy sauce
2 tablespoons white-wine vinegar
1 tablespoon sugar

• Heat the broth, juniper berries, and chile in a large nonstick skillet over medium-high heat, and when they are hot add the cabbage and peppers. Sauté 2 minutes, and then add the soy sauce, vinegar, and sugar. Stir and cook until heated through, about 1 minute.

Per serving: 41 calories, 9g carbohydrates, 2g protein, trace fat

PREP TIME: 15 MINUTES   COOKING TIME: 10 MINUTES

Spiced Shredded Cabbage

MAKES 4 SERVINGS

The warm, sweet flavor of nutmeg will entice everyone to eat more of this vitamin C–rich vegetable.

1 (1¹/2-pound) head green cabbage
4 tablespoons butter
3 tablespoons bacon fat, stock, or water
¹/2 teaspoon flour
¹/4 to ¹/2 teaspoon grated nutmeg or ground mace
¹/4 teaspoon freshly ground pepper

● Shred the cabbage. Melt half the butter in a heavy pot, then add the cabbage and toss until covered with the butter. Add bacon fat, stock, or water, cover, and cook gently until the liquid is nearly absorbed and the cabbage is tender, about 10 minutes.

● Stir in the flour, ¹/4 teaspoon of the nutmeg or mace, and the pepper until blended. Add the remaining butter and toss until melted into the cabbage. Taste and add more nutmeg or mace if needed.

Per serving (with bacon fat): 232 calories, 10g carbohydrates, 3g protein, 22g fat
Per serving; (with water): 146 calories, 10g carbohydrates, 3g protein, 2g fat

PREP TIME (INCLUDES SOAKING): 15 MINUTES
COOKING TIME: 6 MINUTES

Fried Okra

MAKES 6 SERVINGS

This Southern dish is "finger-licking" good!

salt
1 pound okra, thick stem ends trimmed, pods cut
*   into ¹/2-inch rounds*
3 tablespoons rice flour
salt and freshly ground pepper
2 egg whites
vegetable oil for frying

● Preheat oven to 300 degrees. Place okra in bowl of salted ice water. Soak 5 minutes. Line baking sheet with paper towels. Mix rice flour with ¹/2 teaspoon salt and ¹/4 teaspoon pepper in plastic food storage bag. Whisk egg whites in a medium bowl with a pinch of salt until foamy. Drain the okra; blot with paper towels. Add okra to egg whites. Stir to coat. Drain in a colander.

● Heat 1 inch oil in large skillet over medium-high heat to sizzling. In batches, shake okra in rice-flour mixture to coat. Shake off excess and fry okra in oil until golden, about 2 minutes per batch. Place on prepared baking sheet and keep warm in oven, while coating and frying remaining okra.

Per serving: 69 calories, 10g carbohydrates, 3g protein, 2.5g fat

Potato & Sugar Snap Pea Sauté

MAKES 4 SERVINGS

Mashed potatoes never tasted this good, nor have they ever been so elegant!

2 large baking potatoes, peeled
2 tablespoons olive oil
1 garlic clove, peeled and finely chopped
8 ounces sugar snap peas
salt to taste
freshly ground pepper to taste

• Dice the potatoes into $1/2$-inch pieces and dry on paper towels. Heat the oil in a skillet and sauté the potatoes until golden brown and tender. Add the garlic and sugar snap peas and sauté 1 to 2 minutes. Season with salt and pepper and toss to coat. Cover and keep warm until ready to serve.

Per serving: 121 calories, 13g carbohydrates, 3g protein, 7g fat

Celeriac Sauté

MAKES 6 SERVINGS

The straightforward ingredients in this recipe enhance the natural flavor of celeriac, making it a big hit.

1 pound celeriac, peeled and julienned, or 1 jar
  (about 24 ounces) julienned celeriac (about 2
  cups drained)
2 tablespoons butter
1 clove garlic, crushed through a press
1/4 cup fresh lemon juice
salt and freshly ground pepper to taste
snipped fresh chives for garnish

• Rinse celeriac in a colander.

• Melt butter in large skillet over medium-high heat; add garlic and sauté until aromatic, about 1 minute. Add celeriac and sauté until lightly browned, 5 to 7 minutes. Season to taste; garnish with chives.

Per serving: 69 calories, 8g carbohydrates, 1g protein, 4g fat

PREP TIME: 10 MINUTES   COOKING TIME: 9 MINUTES

Roasted Asparagus with Orange Sauce

MAKES 6 SERVINGS

Surprise your guests with this unusual but delicious combination!

2 (1-pound) bunches asparagus, ends trimmed
2 tablespoons olive oil
1 teaspoon grated orange zest
2 tablespoons fresh orange juice
salt and freshly ground pepper

• Place oven rack 4 inches from heat source. Preheat broiler. Line a large shallow roasting pan with a sheet of foil.

• Spread asparagus in a straight line in prepared pan; sprinkle with oil, orange zest and juice, salt, and pepper. Toss to coat. (Keep spears in a straight line.) Broil 4 minutes; turn spears. Roast 3 to 5 minutes longer, until asparagus is tender.

Per serving: 78 calories, 7g carbohydrates, 4g protein, 5g fat

PREP TIME: 5 MINUTES   COOKING TIME: 13 MINUTES

Broccoli with Lemon-Garlic Ricotta Crumbs

MAKES 4 SERVINGS

Broccoli and lemon is always a winner, but the ricotta makes it oh so much better!

1 cup finely crumbled ricotta
3 tablespoons butter
1 clove garlic, crushed through a press
1 teaspoon grated lemon zest
1/4 cup fresh lemon juice
salt and freshly ground pepper
2 cups broccoli florets

• Place cheese in a shallow bowl. Melt butter in medium skillet over medium heat; add garlic. Sauté until aromatic, about 2 minutes. Remove from heat; stir in lemon zest and juice and 1/4 teaspoon pepper. Pour over cheese; toss to coat. Cover.

• Place 1/2 inch water in same pan; season with salt and bring to boil over medium-high heat. Add broccoli. Cover; steam 5 to 8 minutes, stirring every 2 minutes, until tender-crisp or desired doneness. Pour into serving dish; top with ricotta crumbs.

Per serving: 190 calories, 5g carbohydrates, 7g protein, 17g fat

PREP TIME: 20 MINUTES   COOKING TIME: 3 MINUTES

Zucchini Pita Sandwiches with Golden Shallot-Garlic Sauce

MAKES 10 SERVINGS

The pungent garlic sauce turns these baby-squash sandwiches into a feast.

1 *pound baby or small zucchini*
5 *pita breads, warmed and split in half*
2 *tablespoons butter, softened*
Golden Shallot-Garlic Sauce (recipe follows)
olive oil for drizzling

• Fifteen minutes before serving, heat a saucepan of water to boiling. Preheat the oven to 350 degrees to warm the pita bread.

• If the zucchini are very small and tender, cook them whole; otherwise, quarter them lengthways and cut in half crosswise so they will fit into the pita halves. Drop the zucchini into boiling water and cook until just tender, 2 to 3 minutes. Drain thoroughly.

• Smear the insides of the pita-bread halves generously with softened butter and spread with sauce. Arrange the zucchini in the pita halves. Drizzle a little olive oil over each. Serve immediately.

Per serving: 122 calories, 15g carbohydrates, 4g protein, 5g fat

PREP TIME: 5 MINUTES   COOKING TIME: 15 MINUTES

Golden Shallot-Garlic Sauce

MAKES ABOUT 2 1/4 CUPS (10 SERVINGS)

2 tablespoons olive oil

5 shallots, sliced, or 1 large onion, chopped

2 garlic cloves, crushed

2 teaspoons turmeric

1 and 1/2 tablespoons all-purpose flour

2 1/2 cups milk

2 bay leaves

salt to taste

freshly ground pepper to taste

● Heat the oil in a saucepan and add the shallots or onion. Stir and cook for a couple of minutes. Add the garlic and turmeric and stir again. Cook over low heat until the shallots are tender, without browning them. Stir in the flour and then gradually stir in the milk. Heat to boiling and add the bay leaves and pepper. Simmer gently until the sauce is thick. Season to taste.

Per serving: 75 calories, 6g carbohydrates, 3g protein, 5g fat

PREP TIME: 5 MINUTES   COOKING TIME: 14 MINUTES

Sautéed Mushrooms with Pancetta

MAKES 4 SERVINGS

The unsmoked bacon enhances the flavor of the mushrooms, rather than being distracting.

2 tablespoons unsalted butter

1/4 cup 1/4-inch slivers pancetta or slab bacon

12 ounces sliced mushrooms (any kind or a mix)

1 clove garlic, crushed through a press

salt and freshly ground pepper to taste

1/4 cup vegetable broth or chicken broth

● Melt butter in large nonstick skillet over medium-high heat. Add pancetta and sauté until crisp, about 8 minutes. Add mushrooms and garlic and sauté until tender, 2 minutes. Remove to a bowl; season well.

● Add broth to hot pan; boil, stirring, to loosen browned bits. Add to mushrooms and serve at room temperature or add mushrooms to sauce, reheat, and serve hot.

Per serving: 155 calories, 4g carbohydrates, 4g protein, 14g fat

Garlic Cauliflower Purée

MAKES 2 SERVINGS

Even a healthy pile of these "spuds" won't dent your diet. Don't underestimate the amount and importance of visual and sensory satisfaction this dish adds to a good-carb plate. Every forkful should be a revelation!

1/4 cup heavy cream, or more if needed
1 tablespoon butter
2 garlic cloves, crushed through a press
1/2 pound cauliflower florets with stems
salt to taste

• Heat cream, butter, and garlic to boiling in medium saucepan. Add cauliflower; sprinkle with salt. Cook, stirring, 10 minutes, until cauliflower is tender. Purée in pan with hand held blender or in processor.

Per serving: 118 calories, 7g carbohydrates, 3g protein, 9g fat

Sautéed Cucumbers

MAKES 6 SERVINGS

A unique twist on the traditional use of cucumbers.

1 1/2 pounds cucumbers, preferably long English ones
12 thin green onions
2 tablespoons butter
2 tablespoons balsamic or sherry vinegar
1 teaspoon sugar
salt and freshly ground pepper to taste
torn fresh mint leaves

• Heat 2 quarts of salted water to boiling in a large saucepan over high heat. Meanwhile, peel cucumbers and halve lengthwise. Using a teaspoon, scoop out seeds. Cut crosswise into 1/2-inch pieces. Place in bowl.

• Trim onions, discarding root portion and any wilted green. Cut crosswise into 1-inch lengths. Add to bowl with cucumbers. When water boils, add vegetables; cook 30 seconds. Drain in colander; rinse under cold water until cool. Shake to remove excess water.

• Melt butter in large skillet over medium-high heat. Add vegetables, sugar, salt and pepper, and vinegar; increase heat to high. Sauté vegetables until water has mostly evaporated and vegetables are hot and glazed, about 5 minutes. Garnish with mint leaves.

Per Serving: 88 calories, 8g carbohydrates, 2g protein, 6g fat

Braised Radishes

MAKES 4 SERVINGS

Radishes are good raw, but they are excellent braised.

2 bunches large radishes, with leaves (about 12
  radishes)

2 tablespoons butter

1 tablespoon distilled white vinegar

1 teaspoon sugar

1/4 teaspoon salt, or more to taste

1/8 teaspoon freshly ground pepper, or more to taste

1 cup chicken broth or water

1 tablespoon snipped fresh dill

• Trim off radish leaves, leaving 1/2 inch of green stalk. Trim off root tips. Quarter radishes lengthwise into wedges, leaving a bit of stem on each wedge. (You can leave radishes whole, but they will take about 10 more minutes to cook.)

• Melt butter in a skillet just large enough to hold the radishes in a single layer, over medium-high heat; add radishes; sauté 1 minute. Add vinegar, sugar, salt and pepper; sauté 1 minute. Add broth; heat to boiling. Reduce heat to simmer. Cover, but with lid partially off.

• Cook, stirring occasionally, until radishes are almost tender when pierced with a skewer, about 5 minutes. Remove to bowl with slotted spoon. Boil liquid in pan until it is syrupy, about 5 minutes. Add radishes and stir to glaze. Sprinkle with dill.

Per Serving: 67 calories, 2g carbohydrates, 1g protein, 6g fat

Mixed Vegetable Pancakes

MAKES 4 SERVINGS (8 PANCAKES)

We all that know fruit and chocolate chips in pancakes are fabulous, so why not vegetables?

1 (6-ounce) potato

1 (4-ounce) zucchini

1/4 cup shredded carrots

1 teaspoon puréed garlic (2 large cloves, crushed through a garlic press)

1/4 teaspoon freshly ground pepper

1/8 to 1/4 teaspoon salt

1/2 teaspoon flour

olive oil for frying (about 1/4 cup)

1/4 cup sour cream

● Peel the potato and shred into long strands onto a clean tea towel. Roll up the potatoes in the towel and twist over the sink to extract as much liquid as possible. Place potatoes in a bowl. Repeat with zucchini; add to potatoes. Add carrots, garlic, pepper, and salt and toss with a fork until mixed. Sprinkle with the flour and toss to mix.

● Pour enough oil into a large nonstick skillet to cover the bottom (about 4 tablespoons for a 10-inch skillet) and heat on medium-high until almost smoking. Making 4 pancakes at a time, spoon the potato mixture into the skillet in 1 tablespoon dollops and flatten into lacy 3-inch rounds with the back of a fork. Fry until crisp and golden brown in the center, 3 to 4 minutes on each side. Drain on paper towels and keep warm while frying the remaining pancakes. Serve with sour cream.

Per serving: 100 calories, 10g carbohydrates, 2g protein, 6g fat

Sweet & Sour Carrot-Parsnip Julienne

MAKES 4 SERVINGS

Tangy citrus flavorings and a drizzle of maple syrup give this earthy mix of vegetables a lift.

1/2 cup orange juice

1 teaspoon lemon juice

1/2 teaspoon salt

1/4 teaspoon ground white pepper

1/4 teaspoon ground ginger

1/8 teaspoon ground nutmeg

3/4 cup julienned carrots

3/4 cup julienned celery

3/4 cup julienned parsnips

1 tablespoon maple syrup

• Combine the juices, salt, pepper, ginger, and nutmeg in a medium saucepan; heat to boiling. Add the carrots, celery, and parsnips; cover, reduce heat, and simmer until tender, about 20 minutes. Drain and spoon vegetables into a serving bowl. Drizzle with maple syrup.

Per serving: 58 calories, 14g carbohydrates, 1g protein, trace fat

Breads & Baked Goods

Homemade-Granola Pancakes •

Cheddar Cheese Scones •

New Orleans–Style Pizza •

• Garlic Bread Triangles

• Melba Toast

• Parmesan and Sage Fritters

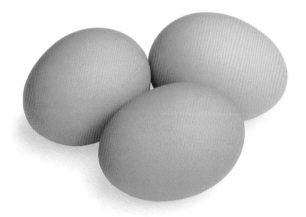

Homemade-Granola Pancakes

MAKES 12 SERVINGS

Toppings for these little fruity pancakes can be as simple as the confectioners' sugar suggested, or you can break out that pure maple syrup or imported honey you've been hoarding. Hot chunky applesauce or melted farmer's market preserves would be soothing additions in the wintertime for a fireside supper.

2/3 cup medium oat flakes

1 large egg, beaten

5 ounces milk

1 pinch salt

2 teaspoons baking powder

6 dried apricot halves, chopped

2 pieces dried pears, chopped

2 tablespoons raisins, chopped

1 tablespoon nuts, chopped (any kind)

1 apple, grated

butter

confectioners' sugar

● Mix all the ingredients together in a medium bowl and let the mixture rest for about 30 to 60 minutes, until the oat flakes swell.

● Heat a skillet or griddle and grease with a little butter. Drop the batter by the scant tablespoonful to make about 3 pancakes at a time. Cook slowly until the edges start to set, about 3 minutes, turn over, and cook the other side until lightly browned. Keep warm. Repeat until the batter is used up.

● Serve immediately with a dusting of confectioners' sugar.

Per serving: 60 calories, 11g carbohydrates, 3g protein, 2g fat

PREP TIME: 15 MINUTES   COOKING TIME: 30 MINUTES

Cheddar Cheese Scones

MAKES ABOUT 8 SCONES

These delicious scones are rich and fluffy!

1 1/3 cups all-purpose flour

1 teaspoon baking powder

pinch of salt

3 tablespoons butter

1/2 cup finely grated cheddar cheese

1/3 cup milk or more if needed, plus extra for
   glazing the tops

1 egg yolk

● Preheat the oven to 450 degrees. Combine the flour with the baking powder and salt in a medium bowl. Add the butter and cut it in using a pastry blender or two knives used scissors fashion until the mixture resembles coarse meal. Mix in the cheese. Mix 1/3 cup milk with the egg yolk and stir into the flour mixture. Roll out to a thickness of 1/2 inch and cut out with a 2-inch biscuit cutter.

● Place on a baking sheet, brush tops with milk, and bake until the scones are golden brown, 25 to 30 minutes.

Per serving: 166 calories, 16g carbohydrates,
5g protein, 10g fat

New Orleans–Style Pizza

MAKES 2 MEDIUM PIZZAS, 8 SLICES EACH

Andouille is a spicy smoked Louisiana sausage. If you can't find it, substitute any garlicky sausage.

4 ounces Monterey jack cheese, grated

1/2 cup sour cream

4 ounces cooked Andouille sausage, thinly sliced at an angle to make large elliptical pieces

2 (12-inch) rounds Pizza Dough (recipe follows)

● Place a large pizza stone on the lowest rack of the oven (optional). Preheat the oven to 400 degrees.

● Combine the cheese and sour cream in a bowl. Spread half the sour cream mixture to within 1/4 inch of the edges of the pizza dough rounds and arrange 6 slices of the sausage on top of each. Slide the pizzas onto the pizza stone or place on metal baking pans. Bake until the crust is golden brown, about 15 minutes.

Per slice: 92 calories, 9g carbohydrates, 4g protein, 4g fat

Pizza Dough

MAKES 4 (12-INCH) ROUNDS, ENOUGH FOR 32 SLICES

1 cup warm water

1 teaspoon active dry yeast

*3 cups all-purpose flour plus a little extra for
    kneading*

1 1/2 teaspoons salt

olive oil

• Place the water in a large bowl and sprinkle the yeast on top. Let stand until dissolved, about 5 minutes. Mix well. Stir the flour and salt into the water and mix until a stiff dough forms. Turn the dough out onto a floured surface and knead until smooth and elastic, about 10 minutes, sprinkling the dough with a little flour when it gets sticky.

• Wash and dry the bowl and grease with olive oil. Place the dough in the bowl and turn to bring up the oiled side. Cover with plastic wrap and leave in a draft-free, warm place until doubled in bulk, about 1 1/2 hours.

• Punch down the dough and divide into 4 portions. Place each on an oiled baking sheet and cover with plastic wrap. Let rise in the refrigerator until doubled in bulk, 12 to 24 hours. Punch down the dough and roll out. Continue as directed with the recipe.

Per slice: 43 calories, 9g carbohydrates,
1g protein, trace fat

Garlic Bread Triangles

MAKES 4 SERVINGS

These are nice crunchy alternatives to potatoes for stews and steaks. Serve the meat on top and the bread will absorb the flavorful juices.

2 thin slices white bread

oil for shallow frying

1 large garlic clove, crushed

• Cut the bread diagonally each way to make 4 triangles from each slice. Heat the oil in a skillet over medium-high heat, add the crushed garlic and bread triangles, and fry the bread on each side until crisp and golden. Drain on paper towels.

Per serving: 34 calories, 5g carbohydrates,
1g protein, 1g fat

PREP TIME: 5 MINUTES COOKING TIME: 2 TO 3 MINUTES

Melba Toast

MAKES 8 PIECES

Melba toast is the quintessential good-carb bread. Eat up!

2 slices thin white or wheat bread

• Preheat the broiler or toaster oven. Place the bread on a baking sheet and broil or toast under the grill on both sides.

• Remove the toast from under the heat, cut in half horizontally with a sharp knife and then diagonally across to make triangles. Toast the uncooked sides until crisp and slightly curled.

Per serving: 8 calories, 2g carbohydrates, trace protein, trace fat

PREP TIME: 5 MINUTES COOKING TIME: 12 MINUTES

Parmesan and Sage Fritters

MAKES 4 SERVINGS (ABOUT 8 FRITTERS)

Sage adds a zesty flavor to these fritters and nicely complements the cheese.

Vegetable oil for frying
2 egg whites
2/3 cup grated Parmigiano-Reggiano or Pecorino-Romano cheese
2 tablespoons chopped fresh sage leaves
1/2 teaspoon freshly ground pepper

• Heat 2 inches of oil in wide sauté pan or saucepan to 375 degrees. Meanwhile, whisk egg whites until foamy and evenly broken up. Whisk in cheese, sage, and pepper. When oil is hot, fry teaspoonfuls of egg-white mixture until puffed and brown, about 2 minutes. Drain on paper towels and serve immediately.

Per Serving: 150 calories, 1g carbohydrates, 9g protein, 12g fat

Desserts

Chocolate-Cappuccino Dream Creams •
Poached Peaches with Chèvre and •
Lavender Sugar
Almond-Berry Fool •
Skillet Cinnamon Tofu Bites •
Tea-Poached Plums with Crème Fraîche •

• Strawberries with Lemon and
Mascarpone
• Jam Bars
• Dried Cranberry & Hazelnut Biscotti
• Mocha Semifreddo
• Chocolate Baked Bananas

PREP TIME: 15 MINUTES   COOKING TIME: NONE

Chocolate-Cappuccino Dream Creams

MAKES 4 SERVINGS

A sweet finish to a meal makes everyone leave the table in a good mood. Most of the preparation can be done ahead of time, so you'll have to leave the table only to put it together.

3/4 cup heavy cream

1 tablespoon sugar

1 (8-ounce) container crème fraîche

1 tablespoon strong espresso coffee

6 amaretti cookies, roughly crushed

2 ounces bittersweet chocolate, grated

• Pour the cream into a large bowl and add the sugar. Whip until it just begins to hold its shape, and then fold in the crème fraîche and coffee.

• Add a layer of amaretti crumbs to 4 small elegant stemmed glasses. Sprinkle with one-third of the chocolate. Cover with half of the cream mixture and repeat the layers, finishing with grated chocolate. Set on a serving plate and serve at once.

Per serving: 407 calories, 20g carbohydrates, 5g protein, 37g fat

Poached Peaches with Chèvre and Lavender Sugar

MAKES 4 SERVINGS

The chèvre gives this luscious dessert a smooth texture.

4 tablespoons dried lavender flowers
2 ripe peaches
4 ounces young chèvre
fresh mint sprigs
1 tablespoon sugar

• Heat 3 cups water and 3 tablespoons lavender to boiling in medium skillet. Cover; simmer 5 minutes.

• Halve peaches; remove stones. Place peach halves cut side down in lavender water in skillet; cover. Poach, basting with lavender water, turning once, until tender, about 10 minutes.

• When peaches are cool enough to handle, peel off skins. Place a dollop of cheese on 4 dessert plates; top each with a peach, cut side down. Insert a mint sprig in the stem end of each peach. Spoon a little lavender water with some flowers over each peach.

• Crush remaining 1 tablespoon lavender with the sugar in a mortar; sprinkle over peaches.

Per serving: 161 calories, 9g carbohydrates, 9g protein, 10g fat

Almond-Berry Fool

MAKES 8 SERVINGS

The almonds and berries nicely complement each other in this good-carb, great-tasting treat.

1 cup mixed-berry low-fat yogurt

1 tablespoon crème de cassis (black-currant liqueur) or a few drops red food coloring

1 cup heavy cream

1 tablespoon sugar

1/2 teaspoon almond extract

1/4 cup toasted flaked almonds

● Whisk yogurt and liqueur in a glass bowl until smooth. In another bowl, beat heavy cream, sugar, and almond extract until soft peaks form when beaters are raised. Fold into yogurt, without blending: you want the swirls to be distinct.

● Sprinkle with almonds.

Per serving: 100 calories, 10g carbohydrates, 3g protein, 5g fat

Skillet Cinnamon Tofu Bites

MAKES 2–4 SERVINGS

Tofu is an excellent dairy substitute; these tofu bites are crispy on the outside and creamy on the inside!

8 ounces firm tofu

1/4 cup dried breadcrumbs

1 tablespoon sugar

1 teaspoon cinnamon

4 tablespoons unsalted butter

● Drain and rinse tofu; cut into 1-inch cubes. Mix breadcrumbs, sugar, and cinnamon in food storage plastic bag; toss tofu cubes, a few at a time, in breading until coated. Place on baking sheet.

● Melt butter in large nonstick skillet over medium-high heat. Fry tofu cubes, in batches, turning gently, until crisp on all sides, about 5 minutes per batch. (Do not crowd pan.) Drain on paper towels.

Per Serving: 186 calories, 10g carbohydrates, 6g protein, 14g fat

PREP TIME: 15 MINUTES   COOKING TIME: 55 MINUTES   COOLING TIME: 1 HOUR

Jam Bars

MAKES 24 BARS

These cookies are fruity and not too sweet.

12 *tablespoons cold unsalted butter (1¹/2 sticks) plus*
    extra for greasing the pan
1¹/2 *cups all-purpose flour*
1 *cup quick-cooking rolled oats*
²/3 *cup brown sugar*
¹/2 *teaspoon salt*
¹/4 *teaspoon baking soda*
²/3 *cup favorite-flavor jam*

• Preheat the oven to 350 degrees. Line a 9-inch square pan with foil, letting the foil extend over the edges. Butter the foil and set aside.

• Combine the flour, oats, brown sugar, salt, and baking soda. Cut the butter into pieces and add to the mixture, cutting them in using a pastry blender or two knives used scissors fashion, until the mixture is crumbly.

• Set aside 1¹/2 cups of these crumbs and press the remainder over the bottom of the pan. Spread jam to within ¹/4 inch of the edge of the pan. Sprinkle the remaining crumb mixture on top of the jam. Bake until golden brown, 45 to 55 minutes. Cool completely before cutting into 24 bars.

**Per bar: 119 calories, 16g carbohydrates,
1g protein, 6g fat**

PREP TIME (INCLUDES BREWING): 15 MINUTES
COOKING TIME: 5 MINUTES

Tea-Poached Plums with Crème Fraîche

MAKES 4 SERVINGS

Fruit and crème fraîche is always an elegant, mouth-watering dessert.

2 bags spiced tea with orange
8 Italian prune plums
1/4 cup crème fraîche
cinnamon for dusting

• Place tea bags in 2-quart saucepan; pour 2 cups boiling water over tea bags. Cover; brew 5 minutes. Remove bags; heat tea to simmering over medium heat. Add plums, cover, and poach gently over medium-low heat until puffed, about 5 minutes. Remove with slotted spoon to bowl; cut in half around the natural divide. Remove skins and pits.

• Place plums and a little poaching liquid on dessert plates. Garnish with a dollop of crème fraîche and a dusting of cinnamon.

Per serving: 62 calories, 9g carbohydrates, 1g protein, 3g fat

PREP TIME: 10 MINUTES   COOKING TIME: NONE

Strawberries with Lemon and Mascarpone

MAKES 4 SERVINGS

Pepper brings out the flavor of fruits like strawberries and pineapple.

1 quart ripe strawberries, hulled and halved
2 teaspoons grated lemon zest
1/4 cup Meyer lemon juice or 2 tablespoons regular lemon juice and 2 tablespoons orange juice
freshly ground pepper to taste
1/2 cup mascarpone
4 lemon twists

• Gently toss berries with lemon zest and juice and the pepper in bowl. Spoon into compote glasses. Top with a dollop of mascarpone; garnish with a lemon twist.

Per serving: 68 calories, 9g carbohydrates, 1g protein, 4g fat

Mocha Semifreddo

MAKES 6 SERVINGS

This frozen treat is a fabulous alternative to ice cream.

1/2 cup unsweetened cocoa powder

2 tablespoons sugar

1/4 cup double-strength brewed coffee

1 cup crème fraîche

1 tablespoon coffee-flavored liqueur (optional)

1 cup heavy cream

● Mix cocoa and sugar in small saucepan. Whisk in coffee. Heat to boiling over medium-high heat, whisking constantly. Boil 1 minute, continuing to whisk. Remove from heat.

● Whisk crème fraîche and liqueur in a large bowl; whisk in cocoa mixture. Cool.

● Whip cream in another large bowl until soft peaks form when beaters are raised. Fold into crème fraîche until blended. Transfer to freezer container. Freeze until half frozen or "semifreddo," and scoop into serving bowls.

Per serving: 153 calories, 10.5g carbohydrates, 3g protein, 13g fat

Dried Cranberry & Hazelnut Biscotti

MAKES ABOUT 3 DOZEN

Biscotti are always such a wonderful treat. Have them with your coffee or serve them with afternoon tea; either way, you can't go wrong.

1 cup dried cranberries
2 large eggs
3/4 cup sugar
1/2 cup vegetable oil
2 tablespoons finely grated orange rind
1 teaspoon cinnamon
1 1/4 teaspoons baking powder
1 teaspoon vanilla extract
1/4 teaspoon salt
2 cups all-purpose flour plus more for shaping
1 cup chopped skinned, toasted hazelnuts

- Preheat the oven to 350 degrees. Soak the cranberries in hot water in a small bowl for 10 minutes.

- Meanwhile, whisk together the eggs, sugar, oil, orange rind, cinnamon, baking powder, vanilla, and salt in a large bowl until blended. Add 2 cups flour and the hazelnuts. Drain the cranberries and stir into the mixture with a wooden spoon until combined.

- Turn out the dough onto a floured work surface and knead 20 turns, sprinkling the dough and your hands with flour as necessary to keep the dough from sticking. Divide the dough in half and shape each half into a 2-inch thick log. Place the logs well apart on a baking sheet and bake until golden brown and firm, about 30 minutes.

- Leave the oven on and let the logs cool 10 minutes. With a serrated knife, cut the logs diagonally into 1/2-inch thick slices. Arrange the slices cut side down on the baking sheet (you may need another baking sheet) and bake until crisp, about 20 minutes, turning the slices over after 10 minutes. Cool the biscotti on wire racks and store in an airtight container.

Per biscotto: 107 calories, 13g carbohydrates, 2g protein, 6g fat

PREP TIME: 10 MINUTES   COOKING TIME: 15 MINUTES

Chocolate Baked Bananas

MAKES 4 SERVINGS

Say goodbye to s'mores! Here are the next hottest things off the campfire.

4 small ripe finger bananas
1/4 cup white-chocolate chips
1/4 cup semisweet-chocolate chips

- Use the last of the coals from barbecuing, or pre-heat the oven to 400 degrees.

- Cut through the peel along one side of each banana. Slide in a mixture of the chips. Wrap tightly in tin foil and bake for 15 minutes.

- Serve in the foil wrapping with a small spoon.

Per serving: 128 calories, 20g carbohydrates, 1g protein, 6g fat

Index